Repetition and the Fullness of Time

Gift, Task, and Narrative in Kierkegaard's Upbuilding Ethics

MERCER
UNIVERSITY PRESS

Endowed by

TOM WATSON BROWN

and

THE WATSON-BROWN FOUNDATION, INC.

Repetition and the Fullness of Time

Gift, Task, and Narrative in Kierkegaard's Upbuilding Ethics

RANDALL G. COLTON

MERCER UNIVERSITY PRESS
MACON, GEORGIA

MUP/ P474

1400 Coleman Avenue
Macon, Georgia 31207

First Edition

Books published by Mercer University Press are printed on acid-free paper that meets the requirements of the American National Standard for Information Sciences—Permanence of Paper for Printed Library Materials.

Mercer University Press is a member of Green Press Initiative (greenpressinitiative.org), a nonprofit organization working to help publishers and printers increase their use of recycled paper and decrease their use of fiber derived from endangered forests. This book is printed on recycled paper.
ISBN 978-0-88146-462-7
Cataloging-in-Publication Data is available from the Library of Congress

Contents

Acknowledgements

This book would have remained an unaccomplished task without the generous gifts of many friends and colleagues. The story of those gifts, of course, reaches all the way back to my parents, Dr. Robert E. and Mary Jane Colton, who passed on to me a love for learning that made such a project appealing and a faith that made me sensitive to Kierkegaard's religious aims and convictions. But here I have space only for a few of the many other names I might mention. Dr. Gregory R. Beabout, for a long time now both a mentor and a valued friend, offered guidance for the original research, as well as essential advice and criticism as the project came into its final form. In the classroom, personal discussion, and his own scholarship, I have learned much from Dr. Robert C. Roberts about the themes of this work, and he encouraged and aided its very earliest antecedents. Msgr. Timothy J. Cronin, Rector of Cardinal Glennon College of Kenrick-Glennon Seminary, provided crucial support in the form of a sabbatical leave that enabled me to find the time and resources for research and composition. Above all, I am glad to mention my wife Kristen and my children, Caleb, Lily Ruth, John, Eli, Mary Hope, and Annarose. Kristen never failed to offer encouragement and share my excitement, even in the difficult family circumstances in which I wrote this book, and the whole family put up with many late nights and distracted moments. The task of thanking all these friends and colleagues for their generous gifts is, for me, a very pleasant one.

To Kristen, because the story of our marriage has shown me that a task can truly be a gift.

moral formation would hardly be recognizable without the use of stories. Any reflective person might wonder about such phenomena, and a philosopher will do so with some particular questions in mind. Why is it we so often make ourselves intelligible to others—and even to ourselves—by telling stories? To what ends can a philosopher put narrative in his own work? What are the limits to the usefulness of narrative for those ends and others?

Recent philosophical ethics has taken up questions such as these with considerable liveliness. Alasdair MacIntyre, for example, has argued that no action is intelligible outside its place in a narrative and that the unity of a human life is the unity of a narrative.[1] Galen Strawson, on the other hand, has insisted that interpreting one's own life as a narrative is almost always distorting and corrupting.[2] But contemporary thinkers are not, of course, the first to take an active interest in the intersection of narrative and ethics; many influential philosophers and theologians, such as Plato, Augustine, Hume, and Nietzsche, have cast their arguments in dramatic or narrative form.

Søren Kierkegaard certainly numbers among this company. Like Augustine and Newman, he offered his readers, posthumously, a narrative of his life and career; but he also makes frequent use of narratives in his many other works. Few philosophers can match him for the sheer number, variety, and artistry of his tales. And since he was unusually attentive to the forms, means, and goals of his philosophical efforts, one might expect that attention to his work can illuminate questions about the philosophical and ethical significance of storytelling.

---

[1] Alasdair MacIntyre, *After Virtue: A Study in Moral Theory*, 2nd ed. (Notre Dame IN: University of Notre Dame Press, 1984).

[2] Galen Strawson, "Against Narrativity," *Ratio* 17/4 (2004): 428–52.

To Kristen, because the story of our marriage has shown me that a task can truly be a gift.

Introduction

I was on a first date with my future wife, feeling a little nervous and eager to keep the conversation going. Hoping to move things along with a little humor, I began telling her some stories about my days as a full-time graduate student and part-time school bus driver in Waco, Texas. It seemed to work: she laughed at the right places, and the conversation picked up steam for the rest of the evening. Years later, I learned that my storytelling had so engaged her not just because, as I thought, it made me look charmingly self-deprecating, but because she believed she was glimpsing something of my character through the narrative. She was discovering who I really was. Since we've been married, we've continued telling stories, both to each other and to our children. We tell them the classic tales of childhood, the treasured stories of our faith, and even about our own upbringings, hoping that they will learn in them something of who they are and whom they might become and so gain practice in better and more praiseworthy forms of life—while enjoying a little narrative pleasure along the way.

Our experience is hardly unique. St. Augustine explained himself to God and his contemporaries in a story, as did Bl. John Henry Newman. Other famous figures in politics, war, business, entertainment, literature, and athletics seek to burnish their reputation or sustain interest in their persons and accomplishments by producing memoirs and autobiographies. And parents have always relied on stories and fables to form their children, just as Jesus employed parables time and again to prepare his hearers for spiritual transformation. Revealing character and identity through self-narration is a constant of our interaction with one another, and the many varieties of moral formation would hardly be recognizable without the use of stories. Any reflective person might wonder about such phenomena, and a philosopher will do so with some particular questions in mind. Why is it we so often make ourselves intelligible to others—and even to ourselves—by telling stories? To what ends can a philosopher put narrative in his own work? What are the limits to the usefulness of narrative for those ends and others?

Recent philosophical ethics has taken up questions such as these with considerable liveliness. Alasdair MacIntyre, for example, has argued that no action is intelligible outside its place in a narrative and that the unity of a human life is the unity of a narrative.[1] Galen Strawson, on the other hand, has insisted that interpreting one's own life as a narrative is almost always distorting and corrupting.[2] But contemporary thinkers are not, of course, the first to take an active interest in the intersection of narrative and ethics; many influential philosophers and theologians, such as Plato, Augustine, Hume, and Nietzsche, have cast their arguments in dramatic or narrative form.

Søren Kierkegaard certainly numbers among this company. Like Augustine and Newman, he offered his readers, posthumously, a narrative of his life and career; but he also makes frequent use of narratives in his many other works. Few philosophers can match him for the sheer number, variety, and artistry of his tales. And since he was unusually attentive to the forms, means, and goals of his philosophical efforts, one might expect that attention to his work can illuminate questions about the philosophical and ethical significance of storytelling.

---

[1] Alasdair MacIntyre, *After Virtue: A Study in Moral Theory*, 2nd ed. (Notre Dame IN: University of Notre Dame Press, 1984).

[2] Galen Strawson, "Against Narrativity," *Ratio* 17/4 (2004): 428–52.

In this book, I intend to provide the resources for fulfilling that expectation. Though Kierkegaard, working in his own time and place, did not directly answer the questions recent philosophers are asking, reflection on his narrative practice can shed new light on them. This light has often been missed because readers fail to begin with Kierkegaard's own distinctive concepts and substantive commitments. Kierkegaard is an unabashedly religious thinker and always writes with a pedagogical aim; he intends to build his readers up in ethical virtue and religious devotion. Contemporary attempts to recruit him as an existentialist, phenomenologist, or analytic philosopher often fail to take seriously his own starting points and goals. In this book, I aim to avoid such oversights by focusing attention on the ways in which Kierkegaard's uses of narrative presuppose religiously accented concepts such as gift, task, and providence and on the pedagogical effects towards which his narratives are always directed.

Thus, my study revolves around the presuppositions, ends, and limits of Kierkegaard's uses of narratives. What substantive philosophical or theological commitments explain Kierkegaard's frequent use of the narrative form? To answer that question, I turn in the first chapter to the concepts of gift and task that play central roles in Kierkegaard's moral grammar. On his account, I can make sense of myself as a moral agent only when I see myself as receiving a gift that is also a task, an actuality that calls me to strive to bring it to its proper denouement. Since this self-understanding requires, in turn, that I see myself as situated in the drama authored by Divine Providence, it can only be displayed in narrative form. God's Providence is a story, and our task is to work with God in finding our place in that narrative and in following the plot to its appropriate denouement. Thus, some of the most nourishing conceptual roots of Kierkegaard's extensive use of the narrative form can be found in his understanding of the ethical life in terms of gift, task, and providence.

So Kierkegaard has plenty of reason in his own distinctive conceptual grammar to indulge in storytelling. But he also uses narrative carefully, with a steady eye toward the effect he hopes to bring about in the reader, and so I turn next to the ends of his narrative rhetoric. Kierkegaard's purposes, even in philosophical reflection, are always pedagogical, or, as he would say, "upbuilding." He intends not just to contribute to a theoretical understanding of moral phenomena but to move his reader towards a better and more faithful enactment of the ethical and religious life. Narrative is especially suited for such purposes, and so one should not be surprised to uncover narrative patterns in Kierkegaard's works even when they appear, on the surface, to be more straightforwardly didactic texts.

In the second chapter, I develop these thoughts by drawing on some aspects of Wayne Booth's "ethical criticism," insights that were largely anticipated by Kierkegaard, to articulate some tools of interpretation that will allow one to discern some of the more latent narratives in Kierkegaard's works and to explain their upbuilding power. Among those tools, I make special use of the distinction between the "flesh-and-blood" authors who ultimately stand behind a text and the "implied" author readers discern as they engage a story, as well as a corresponding distinction between "flesh-and-blood" and "implied" readers.

The third chapter tests those strategies by a reading of some of Kierkegaard's *Eighteen Upbuilding Discourses*. I focus on some discourses concerning gratitude, the task a gift always sets before us. The discourse challenges the implied reader to take up this task and develop the corresponding virtues, thus transforming his perception of giving, of receiving, and even of himself. In doing so, the reader finds his experience figured by a particular kind of narrative pattern, one Kierkegaard characterizes as a "repetition." Following the reader through the ins and outs of such a story makes clear Kierkegaard's pedagogical intentions for his uses of narrative and a certain account of the emotions and of moral development those intentions presuppose.

The fourth chapter probes further the upbuilding intent of Kierkegaard's use of narratives, this time tracing the story of the implied reader in *Works of Love* through another narrative pattern of repetition. Just as the discourses figuring in chapter 3 aim at fostering gratitude in the reader, *Works of Love* intends to build the reader up in Christian love. Of course, *Works of Love* also contains tightly reasoned arguments, arguments about the nature of that love and other closely related concepts. But since these contentions are embedded in a pedagogically focused narrative, I show that Kierkegaard's claims and arguments become clearest when the reader attends to the narrative structure of their presentation. With that structure in mind, certain standard objections lose their force and Kierkegaard's goal of fostering a proper self-understanding in relation to love, authority, and the law becomes manifest.

Finally, I turn to some recent objections to claims for the significance of narrative in ethics, objections that threaten to derail Kierkegaard's project as I have outlined it. I consider some of the more prominent such criticisms, including complaints about the reduction of personal identity to narrative and about narrative's supposed tendencies to self-deception, triviality, hubris, and over-simplification. None of these objections, in my judgment, proves fatal to the Kierkegaardian view I have been expounding, and in the last chapter I explain why. However, I do argue that Kierkegaard himself has some suspicions about narrative and that he sees its limits in its need for a moment that is "the fullness of time." Though Kierkegaard and his pseudonyms provide convincing arguments for the necessity of contextualizing the passing and isolated moment in a larger narrative, they also suggest that the narrative itself depends for its ultimate intelligibility on its encounter with a moment that both belongs to time and transcends it, a moment like that found in certain Christian views of sacraments and in promises, as well as in Kierkegaard's own accounts of joy and conscience.

Kierkegaard's work shows us that the narrative form is not a concession moral philosophy makes to the nursery or to the informal conversation of the unlettered, but is, rather, a powerful tool for refining, improving, and even transforming one's understanding of oneself and of the phenomena of the moral life and helping others to do the same. And he also shows us how to avoid a "narrative imperialism"[3] in moral philosophy by marking out narrative's limits. For Kierkegaard himself, the powers and limits of narrative in ethics must be understood in light of the gift and task with which divine providence endows every human being, and readers sympathetic to his Christian commitments will no doubt be most likely to find his arguments convincing. But Kierkegaard is one of those thinkers who can spark worthwhile insights even when we judge him to be mistaken. So I hope that all students of Kierkegaard, of ethics—both philosophical and theological—and of narrative can find some benefit in these reflections on his thought.

---

[3] James Phelan, "Who's Here? Thoughts on Narrative Identity and Narrative Imperialism," *Narrative* 13 (2005): 205–209.

1

Gift, Task, and Kierkegaard's Narratives

The Grammar of "Gift" and "Task"

Though Kierkegaard often battled against the romantics of his day, he shared with them an intense interest in the arts. And among the arts, Kierkegaard devoted most of his attention to the novel and to drama. His two book-length critical treatments, *From the Papers of One Still Living* and *Two Ages*, for example, deal with novels by, respectively, Hans Christian Anderson and Thomasine Gyllembourg; and Schlegel's *Lucinde* comes in for significant treatment in his dissertation *The Concept of Irony*. In *Either/Or*, the papers of the aesthete include substantial treatments of tragic drama in ancient and modern forms as well as the stories of Mozart's *Don Giovanni* and Goethe's *Faust*. On several occasions, too, Kierkegaard or his pseudonyms turn to criticism of the theater, including a selection in *Either/Or* dedicated to a play about *First Love* and the longer *The Crisis* and *A Crisis in the Life of an Actress*. Kierkegaard himself frequently engaged in more or less complex storytelling, ranging from parables and anecdotes, found scattered throughout his authorship, to novellas such as *Either/Or*'s "The Diary of a Seducer," *Repetition*, and the unfinished *Johannes Climacus*. And this is only a partial list.

But Kierkegaard's interest in his own and others' stories never fell into a romantic idolization of art for its own sake. His chief concerns throughout his writings are always fundamentally normative, and he regularly permits ethical and aesthetic categories to cut across one another. Sylvia Walsh refers to this cross-fertilization as Kierkegaard's "existential aesthetics,"[1] and she effectively shows that Kierkegaard conceived of ethics in terms of aesthetic categories and, in turn, saw the highest development of aesthetic potential in a life well lived.

Why did Kierkegaard, across the breadth of his authorship, allow ethical and aesthetic categories to intersect in this way? And why did he rely especially on narrative art forms? No doubt part of the answer lies in the usefulness of narratives for showing the contours of a human life and for displaying the activity of a virtue or vice. Robert C. Roberts, in a short essay on narrative ethics, describes these uses of narrative in moral philosophy and argues that narrative can also constitute part of the grammar of virtues and vices in a particular religious or philosophical tradition.[2] Noel Carroll has recently attempted to show in more detail how narratives can clarify our understandings of the virtues and vices, aid us in recognizing them by engaging our emotions, and contribute to moral deliberation by orienting our self-understandings.[3] Surely many, or even most, of these considerations moved Kierkegaard to his extensive use of narrative in ethics.

But more can be said, drawing on the distinctives of his own outlook, to explain narrative's pervasive presence in Kierkegaard's work. One profitable place to turn for such

---

[1] Sylvia Walsh, *Living Poetically: Kierkegaard's Existential Aesthetics* (University Park PA: The Pennsylvania State University Press, 1994).

[2] Robert C. Roberts, "Narrative Ethics," in *A Companion to Philosophy of Religion*," ed. Phillip L. Quinn and Charles Taliaferro (New York: Blackwell Publishing, Ltd., 1997) 473–80.

[3] Noel Carroll, "Narrative and the Ethical Life," in *Art and Ethical Criticism*, ed. Gary L. Hagberg (Malden MA: Wiley-Blackwell, 2008; rep. 2011) 35–62. Carroll has expanded this material in a new book, *Art in Three Dimensions* (New York: Oxford University Press, 2010).

further illumination is his use of the concepts of gift and task in ethics. Gift and task, for Kierkegaard, name two termini of the striving and becoming proper to the moral life, and the movement from one to the other is best captured, for a variety of reasons, in a narrative model. In this section, I aim to assemble some remarks articulating Kierkegaard's grammar of gift and task in relation to the rest of the moral life and to show its aptitude for the narrative form.

The Gift Behind the Task. I concentrate on the term "task" because, for Kierkegaard, a task (*Opgave*) always assumes a gift (*Gave*), as the Danish words themselves suggest. Consequently, Kierkegaard often employs the term "task" without the corresponding term "gift,"[4] but such usage does not suggest a conceptual delinking. Kierkegaard instead insists over and over again that every task implies a gift.

Consider the following passage from Kierkegaard's dissertation, *The Concept of Irony*, in which he approaches gift and task by means of a third concept, actuality: "But actuality (historical actuality) stands in a twofold relation to the subject: partly as a gift that refuses to be rejected, partly as a task that wants to be fulfilled."[5] Historical actuality as gift implies the

---

[4] A computer search of Kierkegaard's *Samlede Værker* (conducted with *Kierkegaard: Samlede Værker,* electronic editor Alastair McKinnon [Charlottesville: InteLex Corporation, 1995]; this is also my source for other citations of the Danish texts) reveals 917 uses of *Opgave* to only 494 uses of *Gave,* with the bulk (265) of the latter occurring in *Eighteen Upbuilding Discourses* (*Atten opbyggelige Taler*), which contains three discourses titled "Every Good Gift and Every Perfect Gift Is from Above" ("*Al god Gave og al fuldkommen Gave er ovenfra,*" though one of them omits the first *Gave* in the title). Though not every use of either of these terms represents the same technical sense, as they are both ordinary Danish words, this disparity does suggest something about Kierkegaard's use of the terms: he focuses more on the idea that every task implies a gift than that every gift implies a task.

[5] Søren Kierkegaard, *The Concept of Irony, with Continual Reference to Socrates*, ed. and trans. Howard V. Hong and Edna H. Hong (Princeton NJ: Princeton University Press, 1989) 276.

"individual's relation to a past," the concrete particulars of his historical circumstances. Against the romantic ironists, Kierkegaard insists that that actuality cannot be eliminated and a new one of one's own choosing substituted. Instead the nonnegotiable starting point for every person is his actuality, something he cannot choose or create and yet also without which he could not begin to fashion, in the romantics' own vocabulary, a poetic life.

Why does Kierkegaard resist so strongly the notion that one might create one's actuality? Why does actuality have to be given by another? Insofar as actuality concerns a "relation to the past," one reason is obvious: a past that I create is not really a past for me. In other words, my actuality implies something that precedes my choices, providing a horizon and context for them, and thus something that cannot be brought about by my choices.[6] Further, only an actuality that is a gift could also be a task. To be sure, one might take as a task consistency with one's own self-made actuality. But then one might with equal intelligibility simply create a new actuality each time a new direction suggested itself. If one's actuality is self-made, its perdurance depends solely on one's own commitment to it. But if one's actuality is a gift, then it remains, no matter how hard one strives to be free of it. It precedes one's commitment rather than being constituted by it. "In order for the acting individual to be able to accomplish his task by fulfilling actuality," writes Kierkegaard, "he must feel himself integrated in a larger context, must feel the earnestness of responsibility, must feel and respect every reasonable consequence."[7]

---

[6] Kierkegaard's argument here anticipates moves made by Charles Taylor in his *The Ethics of Authenticity* (Cambridge MA: Harvard University Press, 1991); see ch. 4, "Inescapable Horizons."

[7] Kierkegaard, *Concept of Irony*, 279.

In the *Concept of Irony,* Kierkegaard notes some of the results of the romantics' attempt to use irony to deny the gift-character of one's actuality. Irony, he says, turns history into myth, inventing pleasing romantic versions of the Middle Ages, for instance, in which to try to create its own beginning.[8] Irony teaches that "all religions are equally good" and criticizes others' theses without putting forth its own.[9] All of these ironic twists and turns are irony's attempts to "make room for a self-created actuality."[10] But actuality cannot be self-created; it can only be given, and irony's attempts to evade that fact reduce it to moral and intellectual incoherence.

Johannes Climacus, Kierkegaard's unfinished novel, makes similar criticisms of modern philosophy. Just as the romantics used irony to deny historical actuality and attempt to replace it wholesale with an actuality of their own choosing, so modern philosophers used the acids of doubt to corrode whatever previous commitments the thinker might have and to provide a fresh start, a new beginning. But, as the title character comes to realize, doubt itself must have a beginning, an interest (*Inter-esse*), since it is a "third" that already assumes the relation of mind and world it attempts to question. Modern philosophy's mistake lay in attempting to philosophize—and to teach philosophy—by denying the gift at its base. If not for the gift, philosophy could have no task.

Authority and the Task. Thus every task assumes a gift. This basic insight, developed at some length in these passages, is reflected in a wide variety of other texts, especially when a task

---

[8] Ibid., 277.

[9] Ibid., 278.

[10] Ibid., 275. See also Søren Kierkegaard, *Either/Or*, ed. and trans. Howard V. Hong and Edna H. Hong, 2 vols. (Princeton NJ: Princeton University Press, 1987) 2:258: "The person who chooses himself ethically...does not assume that the world begins with him or that he creates [*skabe*] himself."

is said to be "set" (*saette*) or "assigned" (*anvise*). Such language implies a gift, since the task comes to one from another or from outside one. In *Upbuilding Discourses in Various Spirits,* for example, Kierkegaard identifies the task as "what is assigned,"[11] and ascribes the assigning to "authority,"[12] specifically, the "authority of eternity."[13] As a result, in *Eighteen Upbuilding Discourses,* Kierkegaard associates the effort to set one's own task with the vices of pride or cowardliness, [14] and Judge William, in *Either/Or,* with a kind of futility.[15] In a similar argument, Judge William identifies a "calling" (*Kald*) as a task,[16] and notes that a person who has a calling "generally has a norm outside himself," which, among other things, "often provides him with an occasion to begin."[17] Language associating the task with what is assigned, set, or given thus recurs throughout Kierkegaard's authorship.[18]

In *Works of Love,* Kierkegaard identifies authority with setting the task: "for authority means precisely to set the

---

[11] Søren Kierkegaard, *Upbuilding Discourses in Various Spirits,* ed. and trans. Howard V. Hong and Edna H. Hong (Princeton NJ: Princeton University Press, 1993) 299.

[12] Kierkegaard, *Upbuilding Discourses,* 293. The immediate context describes a child's obeying its parents, but that description serves as an analogy for the human in relation to the eternal. See *Upbuilding Discourses,* 299–300, for the completion of this analogy.

[13] Kierkegaard, *Upbuilding Discourses,* 300.

[14] Søren Kierkegaard, *Eighteen Upbuilding Discourses,* ed. and trans. Howard V. Hong and Edna H. Hong (Princeton NJ: Princeton University Press, 1990) 354.

[15] Kierkegaard, *Either/Or,* 2:294.

[16] Ibid., 2:291ff. In *Eighteen Upbuilding Discourses,* Kierkegaard discusses one's "assigned station," a related concept; see *Eighteen Upbuilding Discourses,* 192.

[17] Kierkegaard, *Either/Or,* 2:294.

[18] For further examples, see Kierkegaard, *Upbuilding Discourses,* 276, and *Either/Or,* 2:302.

task."[19] Nor does Kierkegaard leave the identity of the authority that sets the task vague or unnamed, since the passage just quoted from *Works of Love*, for example, concerns the "divine authority" (*guddommelig Myndighed*). Furthermore, central to the argument of the fourth discourse in the third part of *Upbuilding Discourses in Various Spirits* is the claim that "if God just one single time had demonstrated that he was not love in the smallest or the greatest, had left the sufferer without a task—then for all humankind there is no longer any task, then it is foolishness and futility and soul-pernicious laboriousness to believe, a self-contradiction to work, and an agony to live."[20] If God is not love; if the sufferer is in the right against God who has somehow wronged him; then the suffering constitutes not a task but an attack, and so the sufferer must look elsewhere for a task, a purpose to take up. But where shall he look? In this discourse, Kierkegaard cuts quickly to the chase: if God does not set the task, then no task can be set.[21]

The Nature of the Task. What, then, is the task? In *Works of Love*, Kierkegaard declares of "our duty to remain in love's debt to one another" that, "if it is the task, then of course it must be an action."[22] Furthermore, to be "engaged in the

---

[19] Søren Kierkegaard, *Works of Love: Some Christian Reflections in the Form of Discourses*, trans. Howard Hong and Edha Hong (New York: Harper & Row, 1962) 104. The Hongs, in their more recent translation (*Works of Love*, ed. and trans. Howard V. Hong and Edna H. Hong [Princeton NJ: Princeton University Press, 1995] 97), render the phrase (*thi det Myndige er netop at sætte Opgaven*) "the authority is to assign the task." This latter reading suggests more strongly that the text is focused on the "divine authority" (*guddommelig Myndighed*) just referenced in the preceding clause. Hereafter, citations of *Works of Love* refer to this more recent translation.

[20] Kierkegaard, *Upbuilding Discourses*, 277.

[21] I will address the question of divine authority in more detail in ch. 4.

[22] Kierkegaard, *Works of Love*, 177.

service of the task" is "to be occupied *at the speed of action*."[23] So the task is an action, a conclusion that fits well with Kierkegaard's many uses of the term. For example, also in *Works of Love*, Kierkegaard contrasts the tasks of teacher and apprentice, referring to the teacher who "lectures" and the apprentice who "must make use of it."[24] Elsewhere, he argues that the task of Christianity is "to keep oneself unstained by the world"[25] and that the gossip's self-made task is "to proclaim the neighbor's faults."[26] Johannes Climacus describes the speaker's task as "to express in existence what he proclaims"[27] and the subjective thinker's task as "to understand himself in existence."[28] Judge William maintains the aesthete sets himself a task of "becoming absorbed in his own accidental traits,"[29] whereas the ethical individual seeks to "transform himself into the universal individual."[30] The judge also criticizes an author for having "not comprehended his task deeply enough."[31] Vigilius Haufniensis, in *The Concept of Anxiety*, claims that "each generation has its own task,"[32] and distinguishes the tasks that belong to psychology and to dogmatics by describing the differences in their inquiries.[33] Tasks may also be personal.

---

[23] Ibid., 188 (emphasis original).

[24] Ibid., 48.

[25] Ibid., 74

[26] Ibid., 290.

[27] Søren Kierkegaard, *Concluding Unscientific Postscript to* Philosophical Fragments, ed. and trans. Howard V. Hong and Edna H. Hong , 2 vols. (Princeton NJ: Princeton University Press, 1992) 1:466.

[28] Kierkegaard, *Postscript*, 1:351.

[29] Kierkegaard, *Either/Or*, 2:261.

[30] Ibid.

[31] Ibid., 2:312.

[32] Kierkegaard, *The Concept of Anxiety: A Simple Psychologically Orienting Deliberation on the Dogmatic Issue of Hereditary Sin*, ed. and trans. Reidar Thomte in collaboration with Albert B. Anderson (Princeton NJ: Princeton University Press, 1980) 7.

[33] Kierkegaard, *Concept of Anxiety*, 9, 14.

Kierkegaard refers to his own task,[34] and to Christ's task,[35] just as Johannes Climacus refers to his.[36] Judge William mentions his own task[37] and that of Socrates[38] and of the aesthete.[39]

Considering these examples allows one to articulate more precisely what Kierkegaard means to convey with the concept "task." A task is an action but especially an action characteristic of some person or of some kind of social role or other reality. Thus, the gossip and the one who loves his neighbor can be distinguished by the differences in the actions that belong to their respective characters, just as one science can be distinguished from another by virtue of the differences in the investigative activities proper to each. Such a characteristic action is not simply a brute fact about the person, role, or other reality described but also articulates its purpose. Thus, it is not just that the subjective thinker characteristically expresses in existence what he thinks, but also that he aims at doing so (or is aimed at doing so[40]). Were he not to express thought in existence, he would have to judge himself as deficient, insofar as he considers himself a subjective thinker. So a task represents an action characteristic of a person, social role, or other reality and at the same time a norm, since failure to act in the relevant way will mark the subject as a failure precisely insofar as the subject is identified with that person, role, or reality. One's actuality comprises the gift of being this sort of

[34] See Søren Kierkegaard, *The Point of View*, ed. and trans. Howard V. Hong and Edna H. Hong (Princeton NJ: Princeton University Press, 1998) 118, 119, 125, and the journal entries cited in Kierkegaard, *Postscript*, 2:58, 109, and 117.

[35] Søren Kierkegaard, *Practice in Christianity*, ed. and trans. Howard V. Hong and Edna H. Hong (Princeton NJ: Princeton University Press, 1991) 182.

[36] Kierkegaard, *Postscript*, 1:187.

[37] Kierkegaard, *Either/Or*, 2:219

[38] Ibid., 2:240.

[39] Ibid., 2:182.

[40] See Kierkegaard, *Concept of Irony*, 280–81.

person or filling this sort of social role, identifiable and measured by some characteristic action; one's task, then, is to fully accomplish that action, and so achieve the purpose imparted to one in the original gift.

A task, then, is an action characteristic of excellent members of some kind. But tasks exist at several levels of generality. One often finds in Kierkegaard's authorship, for example, besides mention of tasks belonging to particular persons, virtues, vices, social roles, and so on, more or less explicit references to the "highest task" (*høieste Opgave*). This highest task receives a number of characterizations, depending on point of view and present context.

For example, Johannes Climacus identifies it with "the ethical,"[41] that is, with becoming what one is.[42] Before Climacus, Judge William had already defined the ethical as "that whereby a person becomes what he becomes,"[43] and identified the ethical task as "express[ing] the universal in [one's] individual life."[44] The judge can also be more specific, as when he describes the ethically committed person as one who "possesses himself as a task in such a way that it is chiefly to order, shape, temper, inflame, control—in short, to produce an evenness in the soul, a harmony which is the fruit of the personal virtues."[45] Climacus will later echo this characterization of the ethical task when he notes, citing Plutarch, that "'Ethical virtue has the passions for its material, reason for its form,'" and uses that definition to describe the "tasks that are sufficient for a whole human life."[46]

---

[41] Kierkegaard, *Postscript*, 1:151.

[42] Ibid., 1:130.

[43] Kierkegaard, *Either/Or*, 2:253.

[44] Ibid., 2:328.

[45] Ibid., 2:262.

[46] Kierkegaard, *Postscript*, 1:161; see the footnote for the citation of Plutarch.

Under his own name, and that of his close pseudonym Anti-Climacus, Kierkegaard pushes these descriptions of the highest task in a more specifically Christian direction. To be sure, though, Kierkegaard does not deny the truths in Climacus's and Judge William's formulations. In *Works of Love*, for example, he explains that Christian love requires us not just to love the neighbor but to find the neighbor lovable, "because the task is not to develop one's fastidiousness but to transform oneself and one's taste."[47] Plutarch, Judge William, and Climacus all see the ethical task as, at least in significant part, cultivating the virtues by developing and transforming the passions one is given as a beginning; and Kierkegaard here takes that notion up into Christian discourse, recontextualizing it in the understanding that neighbor love is the bond and perfection of the virtues. In Christian terms, "the task is to love the neighbor."[48] But Kierkegaard, in the mouth of his pseudonym Anti-Climacus, can identify this task even more explicitly with Christian existence: the task is "to become a child again,"[49] "to become and be a Christian."[50] The highest task, then, is fully articulated in Christianity, or, as Kierkegaard puts it in *Works of Love*, "Christianity is immediately involved in the task because it has the task within itself."[51]

The Highest Task and Other Tasks. But the highest task is not the only task, and more specific tasks have their origin in that fundamental one. Immediately before the just quoted statement on the relation between Christianity and the highest task, Kierkegaard writes, "when one *shall* love the neighbor,

[47] Kierkegaard, *Works of Love*, 158; see also 236.
[48] Kierkegaard, *Point of View*, 111.
[49] Kierkegaard, *Practice*, 192.
[50] Ibid., 225.
[51] Kierkegaard, *Works of Love*, 51.

then the task *is*, the moral task, which in turn is the origin of all tasks."[52] And in "The Gospel of Sufferings," Kierkegaard insists that "all tasks have their ground in God,"[53] whose love is the source of the gift at the root of the highest task. Other tasks receive their imperative sense, their insistent demandingness, from their roots in the highest task, a phenomenon Judge William describes in some detail.[54] The multiple tasks belonging to distinct social roles, persons, and other realities derive from the diverse ways in which the universally human is received in the actualities of different individuals.

Of course, one can misunderstand one's particular task, because one can misunderstand one's actuality. Kierkegaard writes, "there may well have been much in existence that had to be cut away precisely because it was not actuality, but it was utterly indefensible for irony to aim its criticism at all actuality for that reason."[55] Kierkegaard here makes the odd claim that much in existence was not actual. What is one to make of an un-actual existence? Reflection on the structure of gift and task as described so far suggests a resolution to the paradox. The beginning point for any given individual, his actuality, may include much that has been distorted by "evil," by "apathy and indolence."[56] One might reasonably take the mark of such distortion to be its resistance to incorporation in the highest task: what cannot be made a part of fulfilling the task is not a genuine element of the gift, for the gift is precisely that which is to be developed in the task. Irony thus plays its important but limited role in seeing through that which merely appears to

[52] Ibid.
[53] Kierkegaard, *Upbuilding Discourses*, 280.
[54] Kierkegaard, *Either/Or*, 2:268–71.
[55] Kierkegaard, *Concept of Irony*, 276.
[56] Ibid.

be a gift but really undermines the task that the gift is for. This kind of "controlled irony" "prevents all idol worshiping of the phenomenon"[57] without denying the gift all together. The aesthete who sees through everything has thus denied the gift and let irony run amok.

One typical way an aesthetic view fails is by confusing task with talent and with luck. "Talent," writes Kierkegaard, "is the indifferent that nevertheless has its importance."[58] A talent is a gift understood in isolation from the task, and so understood as an extraordinary capability available for a variety of contrasting ends. In his journals, Kierkegaard reflected on his talent for persuasion, and then on the temptation to use it for his own cause rather than for God's.[59] Of course, a man of talent will most often put that capability to work for the favored causes of his age, and this is what separates him from the man of genius.[60] The Christian, on the other hand, will be most concerned not with the talent but with what use is made of it.[61] Thus, to build a life around talent is to take the gift but deny the task and so to finally end in incoherence, since actuality is both gift and task. Talent does have its importance; but it is only an aspect of the gift of actuality, which one is to develop in line with the highest task.[62]

---

[57] Ibid., 329.

[58] Kierkegaard, *Eighteen Upbuilding Discourses*, 358.

[59] Søren Kierkegaard, *Journals and Papers*, ed. and trans. Howard V. Hong and Edna H. Hong, 6 vols. (Bloomington IN: Indiana University Press, 1967–1978) 2:1375. (References to Kierkegaard's *Journals and Papers*, here and hereafter, are to volume and entry number.)

[60] Kierkegaard, *Journals*, 2:1301.

[61] Ibid., 6:6748.

[62] Judge William's contrast between "the aesthetic theory of talent" and the ethical emphasis on a calling makes a similar point. See Kierkegaard, *Either/Or*, 2:293–97.

Likewise, in *Works of Love*, Kierkegaard also excludes fortune or luck (*Lykke*) from the task.[63] The poet, he argues, looks to fortune to set the task of love. Perhaps he will find that girl of his dreams to love, but perhaps he will not. The task of love depends on luck. But a task that depends on luck cannot be the highest task, the task laid on every human being and expressing the flourishing of each. So the task of love must rather be set by the divine command, not the arbitrary will of fortune. To think of the task of love in terms of luck is thereby, from the Christian point of view, to suffer a fatal confusion.

Tasks, Virtues, and Duties. Just as the highest task is the origin of more specific tasks, so it is also the origin of duties and virtues. In his description of the highest task, for example, Judge William asserts that someone who has chosen to take it up "has himself as his task under an eternal responsibility, and in this way duty is posited in its absoluteness."[64] Because one has himself as a task, one also has a duty for which one is responsible. One's duty is that which is necessary for achieving one's task, given one's own actuality. Thus, Judge William's focus on duty derives from his characterization of the ethical as a task; task, it seems, is logically prior to duty, a conclusion I have no reason to think Kierkegaard himself would have rejected.

A similar dynamic links tasks and virtues. A virtue is an excellence of character necessary for achieving one's task; and at the same time, the virtues themselves are more specific tasks derived from the highest task. This latter point recurs frequently in Kierkegaard's writings, as he often poses a particular virtue as a task.[65] One may easily infer the former

---

[63] Kierkegaard, *Works of Love*, 51.

[64] Kierkegaard, *Either/Or*, 2:270.

[65] See, for example, *Upbuilding Discourses*, 277 (faith, hope, love, patience, humility, and obedience); *Point of View*, 111 (love of neighbor); *Works of Love*, 55

point from the fact that those same virtues, in Kierkegaard's exposition, gain their significance from their relation to the highest task, as means to it or concrete instantiations of it.

Before considering precisely why this understanding of the moral life in terms of gift and task requires the crosscutting of ethical and aesthetic categories, especially in terms of the narrative and related arts, a short summary may be in order. According to Kierkegaard, our existence—our life as choosing agents—begins with a gift, a beginning point we do not provide ourselves. Thus actuality has a relation to the past; but it also has a relation to the future, because it carries seeds that are to be developed toward their perfection. That relation to the future is the task; it can only be made actual by the action of the agent to whom the gift was given. Thus, the task is to act in such a way that the gift is developed towards its proper goal. Further, if actuality is to be received not only as task but also as gift, then it must be assigned and not self-created; so our moral life must also be understood in relation to that authority that sets the task. Ultimately, God is that authority, and he sets the highest task, variously described as the ethical or becoming loving or becoming Christian. But, given our own particular actuality, we will face not only the highest task but a multitude of more specific tasks grounded in it. As we come to see our moral life in terms of gift and task, we will also come to see our duties and virtues as those requirements and excellences of character that are necessary for achieving the tasks before us, especially the highest task, and that themselves may be the concrete instantiation of it.

(self-denial); *Works of Love*, 95 (attention); *Works of Love*, 236 (love); *Works of Love*, 249 (hope); and *Practice*, 192 (humility). See also *Eighteen Upbuilding Discourses*, 354, in which pride's desire is characterized as wanting to set and finish the task oneself; and *Eighteen Upbuilding Discourses*, 365, in which pride and cowardliness cheat the task.

Gift, Task, and the Drama of Providence

Narrative and Providence. Why does a grammar of the moral life rooted in the concepts of gift and task entail, as I will argue, its narrative structure? One may discern several different kinds of reasons. One sort of argument concerns the goods we prize that only become available to those who can construe their lives as possessing a dramatic or narrative unity. These include forms of decisive agency,[66] intelligibility,[67] self-mastery,[68] and so on. But such arguments themselves depend on some understanding of what narrative is and why it is relevant to accounts of human action, so I will leave them aside to concentrate instead on approaches that focus more specifically on the nature of narrative and its relation to agency.

Alasdair MacIntyre's discussion of the narrative unity of a human life in *After Virtue* suggests one such response. In the course of developing a virtue-centered alternative to the atomistic accounts of action and ethics characteristic of the Enlightenment and its heirs, MacIntyre turns to "a concept of self whose unity resides in the unity of a narrative which links birth to life to death as narrative beginning to middle to end."[69] Insofar as the unity of a narrative lies in the connection of beginning to middle to end, Kierkegaard's description of human life in terms of gift and task has a narrative character. Gift, as Kierkegaard explicitly notes, means a relation to the past; task indicates a relation to the future; and the ethical striving of the individual lies in the middle.

But such an understanding of narrative is still rather thin, and critics of MacIntyre and of readers of Kierkegaard

---

[66] Kierkegaard, *Concept of Irony*, 282.
[67] Ibid., 283, 285.
[68] Ibid., 284.
[69] MacIntyre, *After Virtue*, 205.

influenced by MacIntyre have insisted that they are due a clearer and more precise definition of narrative, one that avoids mere triviality.[70] Anthony Rudd has responded by arguing that MacIntyre recommends narrative as the necessary form for describing *intelligible* actions precisely because, unlike atomistic and scientistic causal accounts, it captures the essential teleology of human action, apart from which we could speak only of efficient causes, not reasons.[71] Kierkegaard's grammar of gift and task resonates with this characteristic of narrative accounts as well. As I argued above, a task is the characteristic action expressing an excellence; as such it provides a goal or purpose for the agent who chooses in accord with it. To describe actions in terms of gift and task is thus to describe them in terms of goals and purposes, that is, teleologically. One might also note that, in general, Kierkegaard's notion of task parallels to a significant degree Aristotle's concept of a function, each specifying the characteristic action of a kind and forming the basis for an account of human flourishing and the virtues.

These MacIntyrean themes provide a solid starting point for a narrative interpretation of Kierkegaard's ethics of gift and task. But I think more precision can be had. To achieve it, I'll begin with some remarks about narrative from a standard, even if not uncontroversial, text in narrative theory, Scholes's

---

[70] For these criticisms, see Jon Lippitt, "Getting the Story Straight: Kierkegaard, MacIntyre, and Some Problems with Narrative," *Inquiry: An Interdisciplinary Journal of Philosophy* 50 (2007): 34–69; and "Telling Tales: Johannes Climacus and 'Narrative Unity,'" in *Kierkegaard Studies Yearkbook 2005,* ed. Niels Jørgen Cappelørn and Hermann Deuser with K. Brian Soderquist (New York: Walter de Gruyter, 2005) 71–89. Lippitt relies heavily on Peter Lamarque, "On Not Expecting Too Much from Narrative," *Mind and Language* 19 (2004): 393–408; and to a lesser extent on Strawson, "Against Narrativity," 428–52.

[71] Anthony Rudd, "In Defence of Narrative," *European Journal of Philosophy* 17 (2007): 60–75.

and Kellogg's *The Nature of Narrative*.[72] Scholes and Kellogg begin by demarcating their subject from drama: "For writing to be narrative no more and no less than a teller and a tale are required." In contrast, "a drama is a story without a storyteller."[73] Drama differs from narrative in that it is directly presented, rather than indirectly presented through a narrator, though it shares other features in common with narrative, such as plot and character.[74] This distinction, to which MacIntyre pays little attention,[75] resonates with one of Kierkegaard's more famous dicta: "Philosophy is perfectly right in saying that life must be understood backwards. But then one forgets the other clause—that it must be lived forwards."[76]

---

[72] Robert Scholes, James Phelan, and Robert Kellogg, *The Nature of Narrative*, 40th anniversary ed., rev. and exp. (New York: Oxford University Press, 2006).

[73] Scholes et al., *The Nature of Narrative*, 4.

[74] Kierkegaard's unfinished and unpublished novella *Johannes Climacus* suggests a similar kind of distinction. Johannes's father makes a habit of telling him detailed stories about excursions through the city; when Johannes learns to do the same, their imagined outings change from stories told him by his father to stories enacted together through dialogue. Indirect presentation gives way to direct presentation. The narrator describes the change this way: "What formerly took place as epic narrative now became a drama; they carried on a dialogue on their tour" (Søren Kierkegaard, *Philosophical Fragments/Johannes Climacus*, ed. and trans. Howard V. Hong and Edna H. Hong [Princeton NJ: Princeton University Press, 1985] 120).

[75] This claim about MacIntyre has mostly negative evidence in support; I'm not aware of any passage in which MacIntyre treats it. Rudd, however, does respond to Lamarque's argument that, because "without narration there is no narrative" (404), most lives (lacking their own Boswell) will have no narrative and so no narrative unity. Rudd's answer is that a narrative self-interpretation does not require a continuous stream of conscious narration (62–63), but he doesn't specify whether he thinks narration always entails a narrator in some sense.

[76] Kierkegaard, *Journals*, 1:1030. See Søren Kierkegaard, *Early Polemical Writings*, ed. and trans. Julia Watkin (Princeton NJ: Princeton University Press, 1990) 78 and the editors' note, 255n97, for Kierkegaard's source.

I will argue that life "lived forwards" has a properly dramatic structure, and that life understood backwards has a narrative structure.

Some of Kierkegaard's harsher criticisms of poetry and aesthetics might make one wonder whether he really thinks human life should be construed as dramatic at all.[77] But that he does so is evident in a couple of ways. Consider his remark in *The Concept of Irony* after noting that, for the romantic, "life is a drama." "What absorbs him," Kierkegaard writes, "is the ingenious complication of this drama. He himself is a spectator, even when he himself is the one acting."[78] Kierkegaard goes on in the rest of the paragraph to unfold the moral defects that proceed from taking up this spectator attitude on one's own life, such as the loss of one's "I," the substitution of criticism for imitation of the inspiring, and a false, merely esthetic repentance.[79] But he never objects to the very notion of life as a drama.

In fact, in a more mature work, Kierkegaard takes up the same image he analyzes in the passage just cited, modifies it, and uses it for his own purposes. In his 1847 *An Occasional Discourse,* the first part of *Upbuilding Discourses in Various Spirits,* Kierkegaard explains the relation between speaker and listener in the context of a religious discourse through the metaphor of a theater performance. Though noting that some might construe the religious discourse in theatrical terms by placing the speaker as the actor and the audience as critical spectators, Kierkegaard rejects this interpretation. He insists instead that the speaker is the prompter; the listener, the actor who speaks within and to himself; and God, the "critical

[77] See Sylvia Walsh's catalog and summary of such criticisms in *Living Poetically,* 169–80.

[78] Kierkegaard, *Concept of Irony,* 283.

[79] Ibid., 284.

spectator."[80] The romantics were not wrong to see life as a drama; they were wrong to identify themselves as both actor and audience.

Other texts also show that Kierkegaard continued to see life in dramatic terms even long after his 1841 dissertation. In 1848, Kierkegaard describes the different perspectives his reader and he himself will take on his own life: "this immensely comic drama [for the reader] is for me a martyrdom."[81] And as late as 1854, Kierkegaard could write of Socrates, "His life is not a drama for men but for the gods."[82]

These passages suggest that life is a drama because it is comprised of a plot and a cast of characters directly presented to an audience. The characters are human agents, and the audience, most fundamentally, is God. And the plot derives from God's providence, as one can easily see in Kierkegaard's discussion of living poetically in *The Concept of Irony*. For the Christian, Kierkegaard argues, living poetically is to "*be* composed"; for the romantic, it is "to compose *oneself*."[83] In other words, the Christian is aware that "life is an upbringing, an education," rather than a project of moody self-expression.[84] One is composed or brought up by God, and so living poetically calls for cooperation rather than self-assertion.

Kierkegaard admits that someone living poetically in a "Greek sense" also recognizes in his life a task, "originality," that provides the necessary context for the exercise of his poetic freedom.[85] But for the Christian, this originality is not only *task* but also *gift*. It is, one might say, the work of providence; and

---

[80] Kierkegaard, *Upbuilding Discourses*, 124. In the image of the prompter, we have again the concept of vocation.

[81] Kierkegaard, *Journals*, 6:6288.

[82] Ibid., 4:4301.

[83] Kierkegaard, *Concept of Irony*, 280, emphases added.

[84] Ibid., 280.

[85] Ibid., 281.

its roots in providence are not unimportant. Kierkegaard articulates the relation between the gift and task of living poetically, on the one hand, and providence, on the other, by distinguishing Christianity's view of God from Islam's. "The infinite negative omnipotence" of what Kierkegaard and his contemporaries took to be the Islamic understanding of God makes the whole world plastic and pliable, "since everything can just as well be something entirely different from what it is," given a divine decree.[86] Nothing has a structure; nothing has a stable nature that makes a thing what it is.

But the Christian, argues Kierkegaard, "knows himself as that which has reality for God," and so construes his upbringing as a development of "the seeds God himself has placed in man."[87] For the Christian, living poetically entails a response to both a gift and a task. The gift has a twofold aspect; it is both the historical actuality, the particulars of the contingent time and place in which one finds oneself, and the "seeds" planted by God in each human person. Those seeds themselves are both gift and task; they are that from which each person starts but also contain in themselves, in potential, the end to which each person is to move, within the context of his own originality.

But all this is the work of providence. Divine providence conceives a plan for the ordering of the world, gives each creature its starting point, and assigns it an end towards which it should move. To put it more poetically: by his providence, God authors the world's story, assigns its parts to his creatures, and works to bring it to its dénouement—a work in which he gives the human creature its own participation.

---

[86] Ibid., 280. For one of Kierkegaard's sources for this reading of Islam, see his discussion of Von Rosenkranz in *Journals*, 5:5222.

[87] Kierkegaard, *Concept of Irony*, 280.

Kierkegaard elaborates this point by way of contrast, taking that popular perception of Islamic theology as a figure for the romantic ironist. In that picture, God's relation to the world is construed not in terms of an artistic plan but rather in terms of brute acts of will. So God can bring about any bizarre actuality he wants, since no such choice could conflict with his own volition, which is the principle of his relation to the world.[88] Kierkegaard's point is that irony attempts to take on this divine role, seeing nothing higher than itself and finding the basis for the validity of actuality in its own whims.[89] Consequently, the ironist lives in a world without structures and so in a world finally unintelligible and incoherent. Kierkegaard thus pins his Danish reader. Like all good nineteenth-century Danes, his reader is committed to Christianity but is also tempted by, if not committed to, the ironic posture. Kierkegaard has now unmasked that contradictory life-view, revealing that the romantic Christian is not just a Muslim but a pretender to the very throne of Allah, and so vulnerable to precisely the sorts of objections Christian theology has posed to Islamic thought.

Consequently, Kierkegaard insists on situating human existence—taking existence in his technical sense as a striving toward flourishing and fulfillment—in the context of divine providence. Doing so reveals its necessarily dramatic structure, its elements of character, plot, and audience. We may and must live our lives forward because they are already part of the dynamic movement of God's providence. We enact this

---

[88] The textbook interpretation of Kierkegaard as the original existentialist in effect identifies his thought with the voluntaristic view he identifies with Islamic theology and rejects. Essence, for Kierkegaard, precedes existence in the form of the seeds divine providence implants in the human person and which the human must develop to arrive at his flourishing.

[89] Kierkegaard, *Concept of Irony*, 277, 278.

movement in the dialectical tensions of our lives; and when we fail to resolve these tensions in choices, commitments, and actions that correspond to God's providential plans for us, we fall into despair.[90]

Gift, Task, and Narratives of Self-Understanding. Nonetheless, it also remains true that we can only understand our lives backward. This backward look at the parts we have played in the movement of divine providence requires *narrative* in the full sense given the term in *The Nature of Narrative,* because it introduces a point of view distinct from that of the audience. Scholes and Kellogg identify three points of view present in any narrative—that of the characters, the narrator, and the audience—and add, as a fourth point of view found in some narratives, that of the author as opposed to that of the narrator.[91]

All these elements are present in Kierkegaard's understanding of how we make our lives intelligible to ourselves and others. Consider, for example, Kierkegaard's own account of his authorship in *The Point of View.*[92] Kierkegaard claims a unity for his authorship extending from its beginning to its end and taking in all its various manifestations, a unity of purpose and end that only became

---

[90] See Scholes et al., *The Nature of Narrative,* 212: "All plots depend on tension and resolution." Of course, Kierkegaard refuses to allow that the dialectical tensions marking our life stories could be finally resolved in a higher, Hegelian synthesis; but this is not to deny a plot to our lives, reducing them only to tension, but instead simply to insist that such a plot cannot conclude before death. The highest task is a task that takes a lifetime to complete just because it is the task of acting out and understanding our life stories in terms of God's claims on us as author and audience.

[91] Scholes et al., *The Nature of Narrative,* 240. They point out that the distances between these points of view open up the possibility of irony in a variety of forms, an insight that could be developed in intricate detail with respect to Kierkegaard's understanding and use of irony, but which I cannot pause to develop here.

[92] See Kierkegaard, *Point of View,* 73–76.

clear to the author gradually and over time. All the parts of his authorship, he insists, were directed to a certain task or mission and unfolded in accord with that mission over time, because God's governance was behind it all. Kierkegaard can see this providential guidance clearly now, even though he couldn't in the midst of the unfolding events. Thus, Kierkegaard as narrator in *The Point of View* knows something more than Kierkegaard as character in the story being told. Of course, the reader, the immediate audience of the story, also shares here in the knowledge of the narrator as distinct from the knowledge of the main character in the story. And God, who is the ultimate audience of the narration as well as the primary author of the plot being narrated,[93] also has a point of view different from that of Kierkegaard as character or narrator and from that of the reader as audience.

Anyone's attempt to make sense of his life could hardly differ radically from Kierkegaard's experiment. I can only make my life to this point intelligible by looking back at it from a point of view necessarily different from the point of view I occupied in acting the story out, and from the point of view of the audience to whom I am making my life intelligible—whether analyst, friend, myself, or, most fundamentally in Kierkegaard's view, God. This latter difference can be plainly seen when one reflects on the fact that the audience can question the narrator's accuracy or intentions in telling the story as well as evaluate his telling of it—and this is true even when the audience for my own narration is myself.[94]

---

[93] Kierkegaard frequently calls human agents "co-workers" with God for just this reason.

[94] MacIntyre adumbrates the critical role of the audience when he names accountability as one of a set of concepts mutually implying one another and making possible the intelligibility of human action. Besides accountability, the set includes narrative, intelligibility, and personal identity; see MacIntyre, *After*

As James Phelan explains, Gerard Gennette has elaborated the concept of point of view by introducing some further distinctions. Gennette argues that the traditional taxonomy of points of view available to the narrator in terms of the grammatical distinctions between first-, second-, and third-person perspectives obscures what is of real interest in understanding the narrator's voice, which is not the grammatical form of the narrator's telling but the "relation of the voice to the plane of the primary story events."[95] Phelan explains that Gennette calls that plane "the diegetic" and has developed distinctions between "homodiegetic," "heterodiegetic," "intradiegetic," and "extradiegetic" voices to delineate this relation more clearly. The distinctions mark the different ways in which the story's voices may be more or less engaged in those diegetic events.[96]

A closely related distinction underlies Johannes Climacus's contrast between objectivity and subjectivity. Throughout *Concluding Unscientific Postscript*, Climacus is concerned with the conditions for achieving or receiving "eternal happiness," the "highest task" for a human being. He assumes that this highest task—achieving the conditions necessary for receiving eternal happiness and living in eternal happiness—constitutes

---

Virtue, 218. Critics of narrative often miss this point, forgetting that the narrator must have an audience capable of putting the story to the question.

[95] Scholes et al., *The Nature of Narrative*, 317. Compare Kierkegaard's use of the traditional taxonomy in a briefly described "Situation" in his journals: "A person wants to write a novel in which one of the characters goes insane; during the process of composition he himself gradually goes insane and ends it in the first person" (*Journals*, 5:5249). Here Kierkegaard reveals his own concern with the relation between the narrative voice and the action of the story.

[96] Scholes et al., *The Nature of Narrative*, 317.

the ethical ideal.[97] Climacus identifies "two ways of reflection" that provide contrasting orientations to the task.[98]

"Objectivity" is the observer's point of view; it is, in Genette's terms, "heterodiegetic," a voice not engaged in the primary events at hand. Climacus finds the paradigm for objective thinking in mathematics and certain kinds of historical knowledge; [99] one might also add certain models of natural science. Common to all these forms of understanding is the attempt to take a perspective outside the realities observed. Climacus notes that objective thinkers concentrate on truth as an object of their study by abstracting from their own relation to it. That approach vitiates ethical and religious commitment, argues Climacus, since, from a perspective outside one's relation to one's highest task, that task need have no more significance than any other. To describe one's "highest task" from a perspective that invests it with no particular significance falls prey to incoherence, since it provides no way to see it as higher than anything else.

"Subjectivity," on the other hand, is the participant's point of view, suggesting a homodiegetic voice engaged with the relevant primary events. Subjective thinkers consider not only the truth to which they are related but also how they are related to that truth. That is, they consider the highest task from the perspective of their relation to it.[100]

Climacus's distinction, then, concerns two ways of understanding one's life in relation to moral and religious

---

[97] See, for example, Kierkegaard, *Postscript*, 1:130–33.

[98] Kierkegaard, *Postscript*, 1:193; see also 1:192.

[99] Ibid., 1:193.

[100] Robert C. Roberts makes a similar point in different terms when he argues that one who thinks subjectively recognizes the "self-implicating" character of ethical concepts, while one who thinks objectively forgets it. See his "Thinking Subjectively," *International Journal for Philosophy of Religion* 11 (1980): 71–92.

norms. But these two ways of understanding correspond to two voices available to a narrator, thus dovetailing nicely with Kierkegaard's dictum that, though life is lived forward, it must be understood backward. Because the actuality of my life is both gift and task, I am always already in the midst of a dynamic movement from a beginning I have received to an end that is set as my task and comprises a particular kind of excellent action that marks my flourishing and successful denouement. Because my life is already implicated in the plot authored by divine providence, it is a drama, directly presented to God as audience. And my attempt to understand my life must take the form of a narrative, in which I recount, from either an objective or subjective point of view, the ways in which my choices and actions have served the plot given to me as a task.[101]

Conclusion

Thus, God's providence is a story, and our task is to work with God in finding our place in that narrative and in following the plot to its appropriate dénouement.[102] This process of learning to understand and inhabit the story of God's providence in our own lives is, in Kierkegaard's terms, our upbringing or

[101] I would also argue here that despair names the lack of intelligibility present in any attempt to narrate my life in alienation from my role in the drama given to me by divine providence, an alienation necessarily present in anyone who tells his life story in an objective, "heterodiegetic" voice.

[102] Kierkegaard does not, however, allow narrative to have the final word. While the moments and episodes dear to the romantic require an encompassing narrative for their intelligibility, Kierkegaard sees such narratives themselves as possible Pelagian temptations. Our narrative, while *contextualizing* the moments of our lives, must also *be contextualized* by the moment of divine encounter, a moment that is an "atom of eternity" (*Concept of Anxiety*, 88) or "the fullness of time" (*Fragments*, 18). I take up this argument in ch. 5.

education.[103] So human existence is a story, a drama, of upbuilding. Kierkegaard's attention to these narrative dimensions of human life should not be too surprising for a reader who takes Kierkegaard's self-avowed role as a moral educator seriously, since mothers, prophets, philosophers, and legislators have always recognized the compelling power of stories in facilitating moral growth or moral corruption.

In Kierkegaard's work, however, these pedagogical narratives often lie beneath the surface of the text and appear clearly only when one looks at them from the right angle. Observing Kierkegaard himself at work in the critical reading of narratives suggests some ways to find that angle. Kierkegaard's comments on reading and readers and his own critical approaches to a variety of novels, dramas, and performances provide the germ for an extensive ethics of reading. He addresses such themes as the traits good readers need (for example, talent, attention, discernment, and care);[104] the necessity of life-view and "governance" in the unity of a narrative;[105] the distinctions between various genres and their relation to human development;[106] the importance of good technique and the reader's appreciation of it; the kinds of defect possible in the novel; and the distinction between the flesh-and-blood author and the author as presented in a

---

[103] Kierkegaard, *Point of View*, 77.

[104] See, for example, Kierkegaard, *Early Polemical Writings*, 68.

[105] For life-view, see, for example, in *Early Polemical Writings*, 76 and, more generally, 53–102; these pages constitute *From the Papers of One Still Living*, a critical review of Hans Christian Andersen as novelist. See also Søren Kierkegaard, *Two Ages*, ed. and trans. Howard V. Hong and Edna H. Hong (Princeton NJ: Princeton University Press, 1978) 12–16, 18–21; for governance, see *Journals*, 2:1455. Note the following claim: "A life-view is really providence in the novel; it is the deeper unity, which makes the novel have the center of gravity in itself" (*Early Polemical Writings*, 81).

[106] See, for example, *Journals*, 1:126 and 1:35, as well as the review of Andersen cited above, *Early Polemical Writings*, 53–102.

narrative.[107] Adequately elaborating all these insights would require another volume, so in the next chapter, I will focus especially on that last theme, drawing on the work of Wayne C. Booth to articulate and extend it.

[107] See Kierkegaard, *Early Polemical Writings*, 81.

2

Implied Author and Implied Reader

Reading Narratives with Kierkegaard and Booth

In work stretching back to the 1960s and culminating in *The Company We Keep: An Ethics of Fiction,* Wayne C. Booth describes some tools for reading that can reveal the narrative patterns structuring many of Kierkegaard's works and at the same time further illuminate the significance of narrative for ethics. Central to Booth's approach is a set of distinctions between flesh-and-blood authors, implied authors, and narrating characters, along with a distinction between flesh-and-blood readers and implied readers. Drawing on Charles Taylor, Booth argues that reading strategies taking these concepts seriously can move the flesh-and-blood reader towards better character. Through a reading of the "Concluding Letter" to *Repetition,* I argue that Kierkegaard's authorial techniques and self-understanding anticipate Booth's distinctions. Acknowledging that the signed works, such as *Eighteen Upbuilding Discourses* and *Works of Love,* pose a challenge to narrative readings, I suggest that attention to the implied reader reveals narratives deeply embedded in both these works.

Implied Author, Implied Reader, and Qualitative Reflection. Booth urges his readers to engage literary works under the rubric of a friendship metaphor. That metaphor leads him to the concept of the implied author, which, in turn, suggests the notion of an implied reader. With these concepts in mind, the reader of any narrative can distinguish between three "voices." The reader first hears the "immediate teller" or "*narrator*," "who takes the whole tale straight and expects the reader to do the same."[1] The second voice is that of the *implied author*, that character whose qualities readers infer from the work as a whole and who suggests that "in responding to *me* you respond to a real person." For example, readers attribute to the implied author responsibility for the possible unreliability of the first voice, thinking of the implied author as standing somehow behind the text as a whole. The final voice is the "*flesh-and-blood person*" for whom the telling of the story is only one aspect of a more complex life.

The implied author, then, exists between the flesh-and-blood person who writes or tells the story and the character or characters who appear in the story. Any readers who have met the flesh-and-blood persons responsible for some favorite story are likely to understand the gap that often exists between the implied author and the flesh-and-blood author. Implied authors, as imagined by readers, may often differ markedly from their flesh-and-blood counterparts, and usually not to the latter's advantage. Often the implied author represents the best of the flesh-and-blood author or that author's aspirations. There is also often a corresponding gap between the narrating character in the story and the implied author. Unreliable or vicious characters may narrate the story without leading readers to infer that the implied author is unreliable or vicious. The actions, sufferings, or transformations of the narrator may,

[1] Wayne C. Booth, *The Company We Keep: An Ethics of Fiction* (Berkeley CA: University of California Press, 1988) 125.

in fact, suggest the implied author's condemnation of the narrator's actions, responses, or character.

As they engage a work, readers form a kind of friendship with the author-character they infer from the work as a whole, so that this second voice gains a certain priority. Booth argues that readers should evaluate that friendship as they would any other, reflecting on it in terms of intimacy, intensity, and so on, as well as in terms of its effect on their moral lives.[2] When they judge their lives with narrative friends in terms of a concern for character, readers must ask, "What sort of character, what sort of habits, am I likely to take on or reinforce as I live that life?" What 'better desires' does it lead me to desire?"[3]

Booth appeals to Charles Taylor's work to explain what he means by desiring better desires. Taylor argues that to be a person is to be capable of "qualitative reflection," of choosing "between goods or desires not all of which really *are* good or desirable."[4] Through qualitative reflection, one passes judgment on one's desires not merely with respect to their efficiency at achieving given goals, but instead with respect to their status as desires one ought or ought not have, "'as belonging to qualitatively different modes of life, fragmented or integrated, alienated or free, saintly or merely human, courageous or pusillanimous.'"[5] Booth concludes that one's engagement with narratives has consequences for one's character because narratives "both depend on and implant or reinforce patterns of desire."[6] Judging and taking responsibility for such patterns in oneself constitutes a central activity of

---

[2] Booth, *Company*, 179–96.

[3] Ibid., 274.

[4] Ibid., 271, emphasis in original.

[5] Charles Taylor, "Responsibility for Self," in *The Identities of Persons*, ed. Amelie Oksenberg Rorty (Berkeley: 1976) 282, qtd. in Booth, *Company*, 271.

[6] Booth, *Company*, 272.

persons. So becoming a better person requires one to become better at discriminating between such patterns of desire and taking responsibility for the presence or absence of the better desires in the self. Since readers ascribe to their implied authors the patterns of desire elicited and fostered by narratives, an ethically praiseworthy engagement with stories depends on careful attention to their voices and a discerning judgment on their values and norms.

Booth also distinguishes between the implied reader and the flesh-and-blood reader.[7] Implied readers accept patterns of desire and fixed norms (that is, "beliefs on which the narrative depends for its effect but which also are by implication applicable in the 'real' world")[8] in a fairly straightforward way. Flesh-and-blood readers, on the other hand, may remain conscious of the story's status as an artifact and the distance of their world from it. But engaging seriously with a narrative work requires readers to take up the role of implied reader during at least some moments of their reading experience. When these two roles "blur" together, stories have their greatest consequence for character.

Implied Author and Implied Reader in Kierkegaard's Authorship. Booth's distinctions have obvious application to Kierkegaard's authorship, and especially to its pseudonymous portion, though I will argue that they also aid us in reading

---

[7] See his description of reading "The Goose that Laid the Golden Egg" in Booth, *Company*, 138–49. Before Booth's *The Company We Keep*, Walter J. Ong, SJ had developed a similar distinction in his essay "The Writer's Audience Is Always a Fiction," the title of which recalls, probably unintentionally, Constantin Constantius's description of his reader as "fictional" in Kierkegaard's *Repetition*. I discuss *Repetition* below. Find Fr. Ong's essay collected in *An Ong Reader: Challenges for Further Inquiry*, ed. Thomas J. Farrell and Paul A. Soukup (Cresskill NJ: Hampton Press, Inc., 2002) 405–27; it was originally published in *PMLA: Publications of the Modern Language Association of America* 90 (1975): 9–21.

[8] Booth, *Company*, 142–43.

non-pseudonymous works such as *Eighteen Upbuilding Discourses* and *Works of Love*. First, though, I need to say a word about applying a tool intended for the reading of fiction to philosophical or theological works like Kierkegaard's.

How can I justify such a seemingly indiscriminate use of Booth's strategies and insights? I might first appeal to the literary character of Kierkegaard's works. Commonly recognized as one of those philosophers most concerned with the literary form of his work, Kierkegaard's writing has drawn the kind of literary attention given to only a handful of other philosophers, such as Plato or Nietzsche. Like theirs, Kierkegaard's authorship overlaps the distinction between philosophical and literary endeavors and requires both philosophical and literary analysis. As I noted above, he casts many of his works in the form, at least partially, of fictional narratives. For example, *Stages on Life's Way*, prefaced by Hilarius Bookbinder's "truthful history of the book," begins with the story of a drinking party and ends with "'Guilty'/'Not Guilty?' A Story of Suffering." *Either/Or* begins with Victor Eremita's story of the book's origin, includes several other stories and reflections on stories along the way, and ends the first part with the long novella, "The Seducer's Diary." *Repetition* is itself a novel and *Fear and Trembling* begins with an "Attunement" consisting of variations on the story of Abraham and Isaac. *Eighteen Upbuilding Discourses*, as I will show in the next chapter, relies on narratives as a central rhetorical and pedagogical technique. Even *Concluding Unscientific Postscript* includes short narratives at key points, and such stories as that of Johannes Climacus's becoming an author or of the excursion to Deer Park serve as more than mere ornamental illustrations. They go further by giving their reader practice in certain patterns of desire and so are appropriate for the kind of analysis Booth describes.

Furthermore, Kierkegaard's use of pseudonyms for certain works also suggests an analysis like Booth's. Kierkegaard, in "A First and Last Explanation" appended to *Concluding Unscientific Postscript*, describes himself as the "author of the author or authors" of his pseudonymous works.[9] Translated into Booth's nomenclature, this claim makes Kierkegaard the writer, the flesh-and-blood author, responsible for characters such as Johannes Climacus, Hilarius Bookbinder, Constantin Constantius, and so on. These characters themselves narrate the works in which they figure, making Kierkegaard, in his own terms, the author of the authors. Kierkegaard does not explicitly make the further distinction between the pseudonymous characters and the implied author of each of the works, but it easily follows from the form of his authorship. His pseudonyms, for instance, are obviously invented names, so one should not imagine that even his contemporaries believed Hilarius Bookbinder or Nicolaus Notabene to be flesh-and-blood persons.[10] Instead, they took those characters just as characters and inferred from each work a picture of the author responsible for the character and his narration. That picture is the implied author. Kierkegaard asks that the pseudonymous works be attributed to the

---

[9] Kierkegaard, *Postscript*, 1:[627]. The brackets indicate that the page in question was unnumbered in Kierkegaard's Danish text, though the Hongs supply the number in brackets for the reader of their English translation.

[10] See Kierkegaard, *Postscript*, 1:[625]; Merold Westphal, *Becoming a Self: A Reading of Kierkegaard's* Concluding Unscientific Postscript (West Lafayette IN: Purdue University Press, 1996) 8–9; and the letters from Danish contemporaries of Kierkegaard detailing news and views of his recently, though pseudonymously, published *Either/Or*, collected in Bruce Kirmmse, *Encounters with Kierkegaard: A Life as Seen by His Contemporaries*, trans. Bruce H. Kirmmse and Virginia R. Laursen (Princeton NJ: Princeton University Press, 1996) 57–59.

pseudonyms themselves and not to him. If not for the unavoidable convention of referring to implied authors by the names of their writers, he might have asked for commentators to attribute the pseudonyms' claims to the implied authors of their works, since they themselves are narrating characters within productions whose totality implies another person.

In *The Point of View*, Kierkegaard comes nearer to an explicit use of the notion of an implied author, distinguishing between his "private character" and his "author-character."[11] His private character is his flesh-and-blood person; his author-character is the person he intended to imply by the totality of each work and of the authorship as a whole. His recognition that his private character "for me contains much of the explanation of my author-character"[12] anticipates some of Booth's comments on the relation between implied author and writer.[13] But in *The Point of View* Kierkegaard also worries that those who would draw wrong inferences from the material may miss the person he intends to imply by his entire authorship.[14] He intended for his readers to infer not just the qualities of the implied authors of various works but also the implied author of the corpus as a whole. In his self-commentary, he claims to have carefully planned his works so as to prevent any good reader from inferring that his

---

[11] Kierkegaard, *Point of View*, 26.

[12] Ibid.

[13] See, for example, Booth, *Company*, 128–29.

[14] This concern requires yet another distinction, that between the implied author of a single work and the "career author." Booth describes the career author as the "cumulative character whom we infer as we read a second or third tale told by what we call the 'same' teller" (Booth, *Company*, 150). Booth discusses the difficulties his students have in appreciating John Milton's careful efforts to create a career author through the methodical mastering of successive poetic forms and subjects (Booth, *Company*, 129). Kierkegaard is an even more striking example of someone who thinks of his creation of a career author in self-conscious ways.

religiousness came only with age.[15] One may conclude, then, that Kierkegaard was very much aware of the distinctions between implied author, narrator, and writer.

Besides his reflections on his own authorship, one may also see that awareness in his comments about the reader of his works. Describing the phenomenon of reading with the concepts of writer, narrator, and implied author attributes a great deal of activity to readers. Of course, one need not think of readers in this way. One might think of readers as passive in the act of reading, merely receiving ideas or images, and becoming active only after they finish reading, as they consider what they should do or think about what they have passively received. But Kierkegaard, like Booth, regards the reader as an active participant in the transaction with the author. For example, the preface to the *Four Upbuilding Discourses* of 1843 credits the good reader with transforming the text, the reader "who in receiving it does for it by himself and by his acceptance what the temple box did by itself for the widow's mite: sanctifies the gift, gives it meaning, and transforms it into much."[16]

Kierkegaard is looking for a certain kind of reader, the one he calls "favorably disposed" and "*my* reader."[17] The reader the implied (career) author expects we may call the "implied reader." In Kierkegaard's published works, Constantin Constantius provides one of the most explicit articulations of the concepts of both implied author and implied reader. The last section of *Repetition*, "Concluding Letter by Constantin Constantius," begins by addressing the reader. "*My dear Reader*! Forgive me for addressing you so familiarly, but we

---

[15] Kierkegaard, *Point of View*, 30–31. See pp. 71–77 for Providence's role in this plan.

[16] Kierkegaard, *Eighteen Upbuilding Discourses*, 107.

[17] Ibid. and elsewhere throughout the authorship.

are, after all, *unter uns* [by ourselves]. Although you are indeed fictional, you are by no means a plurality to me but only one, and therefore we are just you and I."[18] By describing the reader as "fictional," Constantin identifies his addressee as the implied reader.

In the next paragraph, Constantin introduces the concept of a "genuine reader," one who has learned "that it is an art to be a good reader,"[19] to fully engage the work in the proper way. Constantin identifies his implied reader with the genuine reader in the third paragraph, in which he describes a number of contrasting poor readers. He depicts such characters as "an inquisitive female reader," a "concerned family man," a "temporary genius," a "convivial family friend," a "vigorous champion of actuality," an "experienced matchmaking woman," and "His Reverence."[20] In the final sentence of that paragraph, he enlists the implied reader in his disapproval of those false readers, commenting, "My dear reader, we certainly may speak this way about these matters *unter uns*."[21] Constantin has formed an intimate friendship with the implied reader that enables him to speak with the reader "just between us." Their friendship includes common judgments and agreement on aesthetic or technical norms (since genuine reading is an "art") and moral norms (since his critiques of false readers center on their inadequate concerns). These are, in Booth's terms, "fixed norms," the realities Constantin expects his reader to find both in the world of the novel and in the reader's larger world, in which reading *Repetition* is only a

---

[18] Søren Kierkegaard, *Fear and Trembling/Repetition*, ed. and trans. Howard V. Hong and Edna H. Hong (Princeton NJ: Princeton University Press, 1983) 225, emphasis and brackets in original. (Cited hereafter as *Repetition*.)

[19] Kierkegaard, *Repetition*, 225.

[20] Ibid., 225–26.

[21] Ibid., 225.

moment. Not only does Constantin count on his implied reader's grasp of the appropriate aesthetic and moral norms, he also depends on the implied reader's penetrating insight into his characters' psychology. Constantin says to the reader, "you understand the interior psychic states and emotions, and that is why I call you 'dear.'"[22] This piece of flattery may make most clear the difference between the implied reader and the flesh-and-blood reader, since for many readers the descriptions of psychological states in *Repetition*—such as repetition itself, "the raising of his consciousness to the second power"[23]—remain less than pellucid.

But Constantin's comments about the young man may also make many readers aware of the difference between themselves and the implied reader. In the "Concluding Letter," Constantin tells the reader, "The young man I have brought into being is a poet."[24] To this point in the book, the reader has had no indication that the young man is Constantin's creation. The surprise that many, if not most, readers experience at this revelation subverts any inclination they might have had to identify themselves directly with Constantin's implied reader. Constantin's nonchalance suggests the implied reader would already have realized the truth about Constantin's relation to the young man. Constantin's revelation also underscores the distinction between narrator and author. In the novel, both Constantin's voice and the young man's narrate. The "Concluding Letter" instructs the reader to identify the young man as merely a narrating character and Constantin as the author. But, of course, all along most readers will already have identified Constantin as a narrating character in a fiction

[22] Ibid., 231.
[23] Ibid., 229.
[24] Ibid., 228.

devised by the flesh-and-blood Kierkegaard and will already have inferred the qualities of the implied Kierkegaard. Constantin's implied reader, then, is not the flesh-and-blood reader of the work, since Constantin's implied reader seems to know nothing of Kierkegaard or even of Constantin's own fictional status. But neither is Constantin's implied reader Kierkegaard's implied reader, who, one assumes, knows well enough all along to take the novel's letters as imaginative creations and not as historical documents. Constantin's literary shenanigans remind readers that a gap always exists not just between the implied author and the flesh-and-blood author but also between themselves and the implied reader. In Constantin's case, of course, that implied reader is sophisticated, perceptive, and morally impressive—and most flesh-and-blood readers will surely have trouble measuring up to such a high standard.

But the distinction between flesh-and-blood and implied readers can also blur in the reading of a text. In *The Company We Keep*, Booth provides an example of the overlap between flesh-and-blood and implied reader. "If I have revelled in Rocky's battering of the brutish Soviet slugger,...the physical pleasure in the images of bloody bashing has become not just some 'implied reader's' but mine."[25] Here the blurring is obvious because "physical pleasure" requires a flesh-and-blood body, something the implied reader lacks. But it occurs in less obvious ways as well. Speaking of *Finnegan's Wake*, Booth writes,

> Stopping after two paragraphs, I may, of course, choose not to read any more of this giant of a novel. But if I do go on, it will be because I desire more of "this," whatever this kind of companionship is. ...In short, the shaping of my desires will

[25] Booth, *Company*, 295.

> occur.... Unless I am made to want *something*, I stop reading. Notice again that in this one kind of activity, the journey toward a desired reward, the distinction between what the implied reader does and the flesh-and-blood reader does becomes blurred.[26]

Consequently, for the attentive and disciplined reader, reading the text becomes a means for the development, shaping, and reinforcing of desires and concerns.

Reflection on the reading experience also provides opportunity for the kind of qualitative reflection Booth describes. Most of Kierkegaard's authorship takes the form it does to lead the reader through the shaping of desire and the qualitative reflection reading makes possible. One may plausibly construe his whole authorship as an attempt to make his readers aware of the qualitative distinctions between different modes of life and to take responsibility for their choices with respect to those distinctions.[27]

It is not surprising, then, that Kierkegaard grasps and makes ingenious and sophisticated use of the concepts Booth articulates. But one may still object that Booth's distinctions apply to Kierkegaard's works only in those pseudonymous works that most resemble fictional narratives. Kierkegaard signed his name to *Eighteen Upbuilding Discourses* and to *Works of Love*, and they seem neither fictional nor narrative. So I must still make a case for the use of these reading strategies with respect to the *Discourses* and *Works of Love*.

Implied Narratives in Eighteen Upbuilding Discourses *and* Works of Love. Since Kierkegaard's signed works bear his own name, one might take them to report his own ideas and convictions. But if one attempts to describe the implied authors

---

[26] Ibid., 204–205, emphasis in original.
[27] Kierkegaard, *Point of View*, 50–51.

of works as various as *Eighteen Upbuilding Discourses, For Self-Examination,* and the articles first translated into English as *Attack Upon "Christendom,"* one fails to come up with a single, unified portrait. From *Eighteen Upbuilding Discourses,* one may infer an author who is morally serious in a religiously generic way, someone who has a deep concern for his relationship to God. He is intelligent, creative, and subtle, and always aware of the implications of genuinely religious concepts for a human life. His orientation is to those truths any religious person might acknowledge, though his texts and contexts are Christian. The implied author of *For Self-Examination* appears similar in his intelligence and subtlety, but with a new, passionate concern for the person of Christ and for the state of his followers. One notes, as instances of his specifically Christian passions, that he cultivates in himself and his reader a heightened awareness of the meaning of Christ's ascension and of the Spirit's descent. *Attack Upon "Christendom"* suggests an author differing from the first even more. From it, one may infer an author who has an intense concern for the welfare of Christianity in its concrete manifestations. He is intelligent and creative, but his subtlety reveals itself in biting wit and bitter sarcasm. He is not, like the author of *Eighteen Upbuilding Discourses,* a gentle teacher, or, like the author of *For Self-Examination,* a Christian exhorter. Instead, he is forceful, polemical, attacking the entire established order and the individuals who work within it. Any attempt to take one of these implied authors as the best picture one can form of the "true" Kierkegaard fails. Each is a moment in the life of the career author to be inferred from all of Kierkegaard's works. So, if one takes Kierkegaard's signature as simply guaranteeing that the author one infers from the work is Kierkegaard, one will miss the point. Thus, even Kierkegaard's signed works require something like Booth's distinction between implied author and writer.[28] But more needs to be said about *Eighteen Upbuilding Discourses* and *Works of Love* in particular.

Of the two, *Eighteen Upbuilding Discourses* offers less resistance to a narrative strategy. Consider the four upbuilding discourses published together in December 1843 and, especially, the third discourse within that set. These discourses invite narrative reading strategies in three ways: first, their theme, announced in the first discourse, concerns the virtues of Job, who receives his world restored after losing it all; second, the pattern of Job's life echoes the plot of the novel *Repetition*, published just a few weeks earlier; finally, the third discourse employs a series of small vignettes as a pedagogical strategy meant to aid the reader's growth in virtue. Kierkegaard adopts the unusual strategy of telling these stories in the second person, drawing the flesh-and-blood readers into the kind of reflection that facilitates moral development by identifying them with the implied reader. The textual identification reveals more sharply the divergence between flesh-and-blood and implied readers, since in the larger world the identification does not hold as securely. These discourses, then, have their own narrative background and require narrative reading strategies because of their direct engagement of the implied reader. In the next chapter, I provide a more complete narrative reading of the third discourse.

---

[28] Booth writes, "[T]he distinction between genuine literature...and...'didactic' literature is entirely misleading if it suggests that some stories, those that we seem to read just for enjoyment, are purged of all teaching" (Booth, *Company*, 151–52). Of course, to claim that every narrative teaches is not also to claim that every teaching is a narrative. Nonetheless, Booth's argument for the didactic character of all stories does give us some reason to resist the claim that one should not read philosophical works with skills learned from the reading of narratives.

Works of Love poses a more difficult challenge for narrative reading strategies. But careful attention to the reader implied by the text uncovers a story of the reader's growth in love that constitutes an organizing principle for the book. In the preface affixed to both series of deliberations, Kierkegaard describes the implied reader at some length.

> These Christian deliberations, which are the fruit of much deliberation, will be understood slowly but then also easily, whereas they will surely become very difficult if someone by hasty and curious reading makes them very difficult for himself. *That single individual* who first deliberates within himself whether or not he will read, if he then chooses to read, will lovingly deliberate whether the difficulty and the ease, when placed thoughtfully together on the scale, relate properly to each other so that what is essentially Christian is not presented with a false weight by making the difficulty or by making the ease too great.[29]

The implied reader is intentional, deliberate, slow, and well-informed with respect to the essentially Christian. "*That single individual*" reads for himself, not for any crowd. The preface also suggests that the implied reader will accurately judge the adequacy of Kierkegaard's presentation of the essentially Christian. But a favorably disposed reader who finishes the work will probably find that this expectation is reversed in the process, as he finds the law of love the book explicates judging him instead. Just as *Repetition* works to undo the reader's self-congratulation, so *Works of Love* will puncture the reader's self-justification.

That reversal suggests that the implied reader is also a character in a narrative. His progress towards the love the law commands provides the narrative that structures the first series

[29] Kierkegaard, *Works of Love*, 3, emphasis in original.

of deliberations. First he learns the internal connection between faith, love, and the works of love (Deliberation I), which prepares him, as a professing Christian, to desire love. Then he learns to distinguish preferential love from neighbor love (IIA). Aware of the distinction, he must learn to dethrone preferential love (IIB) and develop a new moral vision that recontextualizes his prior concerns and commitments (IIC). From his new perspective he is confronted with his guilt and Christ's fulfillment of the law he fails to obey (IIIA). Finally, he begins really to grasp the possibility of loving from a pure heart and a sincere faith, a possibility that opens up the depths of love (IIIB). But then he must face the hard reality: that possibility comes to pass only if he learns to love the people he sees, that is, to see his neighbor as lovable (IV). And the lesson of the last deliberation in the series is simply that the lessons never end in this life. Love requires him to remain in love's debt with his neighbor (V). Finally, in the conclusion to the work as a whole, Kierkegaard presents the Apostle John as one at the final stage of such a narrative, in which love has become second nature. In the fourth chapter, I offer a reading of *Works of Love* that clarifies the concepts of faith, love, and authority at work in the text by close attention to this narrative of the implied reader's upbringing in Christian love.

3

Repetition, Emotion, and Moral Development in Kierkegaard's Pedagogical Narratives

The *Four Upbuilding Discourses* of 1843

Introduction

In December 1843, Kierkegaard published a volume of four upbuilding discourses. The first discourse proposes Job's life as an ethical-religious paradigm because he had the faith, patience, and gratitude to receive again as a gift what had been taken from him in his sufferings.[1] The next three show how those virtues can make possible a similar recovery of what has been lost for the discourses' reader, employing a narrative pattern identified in some of Kierkegaard's works as a "repetition." But they aim at more than description. They intend to "win" or "move" their reader to a genuinely religious existence and especially to the virtues most central to Job's exemplarity.[2] In the third discourse, for example, repetition appears as a rhetorical strategy in thirteen short narratives, and the attention paid to the virtues of giving and receiving reinforce the nature of repetition itself as a gift. By moving the

---

[1] See George Pattison, "'Who' Is the Discourse? A Study in Kierkegaard's Religious Literature," *Kierkegaardiana* 16 (1993): 28–45, for a discussion of the personification of the discourse in Kierkegaard's upbuilding discourses.

[2] See Kierkegaard, *Journals*, 1:641. For a similar claim, see Andrew J. Burgess, "Patience and Expectancy in Kierkegaard's Upbuilding Discourses," in *Kierkegaard Studies: Yearbook*, ed. Niels Jørgen Cappelørn, Hermann Dueser, and Jon Stewart (Berlin/New York: Walter de Gruyter, 2000) 217.

reader to self-reflection through engagement in a narrative pattern of repetition, Kierkegaard aims at a pedagogical effect. This chapter focuses on the third discourse's narratives to illuminate both Kierkegaard's purpose in employing the narrative form and the importance of that form for some of his substantive commitments about the nature of the emotions and of moral development.

Each of the upbuilding discourses aims to cultivate properly religious concerns in the reader and to clarify the concepts with which the reader grasps the objects of those concerns. This task is a central one for a religious discourse because one can reliably and accurately see the significance of oneself and one's world only when one sees them in the light of the proper objects of concern, religiously understood. When one grasps those objects of concern under faulty concepts, one is liable to lose them and, with them, one's sense of the meaning of one's world. Getting that meaning back by acquiring a more adequate conceptual grasp of one's objects of concern—i.e., coming to see oneself and one's world accurately by seeing their significance in relation to proper objects of concern understood in the most adequate way—is a crucial part of becoming religiously virtuous. Since to construe one's world on the basis of one's concerns is, arguably, to experience an emotion, becoming virtuous also entails a transition to more appropriate emotional responses. Because they are finally received as gifts, such transitions form a trajectory best described in narrative form; they come contingently, sometimes surprisingly, rather than necessarily. These three claims—that reliable and accurate moral perception depends on a repetition, that moral perception is or can be an emotional response, and that the development of proper emotions takes the form of a narrative—provide the focal points for my reading of the third discourse.

The four sections of this chapter consider the discourse's context and pedagogical aims, as well as its implications for accounts of the emotions and moral development. The first section sets the context for reading the third discourse by describing the relation between the Job discourse and the other three. The second section details the third discourse's use of narratives of repetition and their pedagogical effect, while the third section clarifies the implied account of the emotions. The final section argues that a narrative model of moral development best fits the process of becoming religiously virtuous.

The *Four Upbuilding Discourses* of 1843

Kierkegaard takes as his title for the first discourse the latter part of the verse that he also takes as his text: "The Lord gave, and the Lord took away; blessed be the name of the Lord." This sentence of Job's, Kierkegaard's discourse notes, has become a proverb everyone knows and repeats, passing it down through the generations. But it alone does not make Job "the teacher of humankind" everyone knows he is,[3] nor will that kind of repetition encourage anyone in the right way. One may properly call Job a teacher of humankind, not because he has left behind a proverb but because he has "left only himself as a prototype, his life as a guide for everyone."[4] Job's exemplarity lies in his struggle to recover what he had lost, overcoming doubt with faith, ingratitude with thankfulness, and impatience with long-suffering. Job's task, and the concepts that shape his responses to testing, form the context for the

[3] Kierkegaard, *Eighteen Upbuilding Discourses*, 109.
[4] Ibid.; cf. 112.

three accompanying discourses and for the pedagogical strategies Kierkegaard pursues in them by means of the narrative form.

Job's struggle, as recounted in the first discourse, began when he was informed by several messengers that he had lost everything he valued most, including even his children, the source of his greatest joy.[5] With these losses, Job was in danger of losing himself, a possibility the discourse describes in arresting images: Job might have been "starved out in the insatiable craving of the lack";[6] consumed by the "worm of craving that would not die in his soul";[7] wasted "in a demented possession of what had been lost";[8] or he might have "[thrown] himself away" or become a "wanton."[9]

As I noted in the last chapter, just a few weeks before publishing these upbuilding discourses, Kierkegaard had published pseudonymously another short work, *Repetition: A Venture in Experimenting Psychology,* which explores some of the same disturbing possibilities as the Job discourse.[10] Letters from a young man to an older adviser, in which he expresses his despair at losing his beloved, comprise portions of the book. Noting the same text that the discourse expounds, the young man calls on Job as a fellow sufferer, imagining Job as

---

[5] Ibid., 114.

[6] Ibid., 117.

[7] Ibid.

[8] Ibid., 118.

[9] Ibid.

[10] See Edward Mooney, "*Repetition*: Getting the World Back," in *The Cambridge Companion to Kierkegaard,* ed. Alastair Hannay and Gordon D. Marino (Cambridge: Cambridge University Press, 1997) 282–307; and "Getting the World Back: Kierkegaard on the *Book of Job,*" in *Selves in Discord and Resolve: Kierkegaard's Moral-Religious Psychology from* Either/Or *to* Sickness Unto Death (New York/London: Routledge, 1996) 27–40, for lucid discussions of the themes in the Job discourse and *Repetition.*

an advocate for him in his own suffering.[11] Though surely the reader should not take at face value the young man's equation of his own suffering with Job's, the young man's description of his loss of self captures vividly the possibilities that the discourse notes only in the third person. The young man laments, "I am nauseated by life; it is insipid—without salt and meaning. ...One sticks a finger into the ground to smell what country one is in; I stick my finger into the world—it has no smell. Where am I? What does it mean to say: the world? What is the meaning of that word? Who am I?"[12] The young man has lost his beloved and, worse still, finds himself cast as the guilty party even though he remains utterly convinced of his own innocence. In such an experience, the concerns by which he had previously oriented himself in the world fail to provide significance and direction to his choices and responses, rendering him immobilized.[13] At the end of the letter containing this lament, he cites a catechism's definition of "world": "As a rule, the word 'world' includes both heaven and earth and everything found therein."[14] Unfortunately, the young man cannot find himself in the world, since the cares and concerns that previously attached him to the world in particular ways have dissolved. He has lost sight of the value

---

[11] Kierkegaard, *Repetition*, 197.

[12] Ibid., 200.

[13] Ibid., 214. Stephen Crites argues that the passage referred to here, beginning "I am inside," should be translated, "Here I sit." The latter better pictures the young man's claim at the end of the paragraph that he has remained "for a whole month now, without moving a foot or making one single movement" (Kierkegaard, *Repetition*, 214), and more vividly captures the loss of his world that threatens the young man. See Stephen Crites, "'The Blissful Security of the Moment': Recollection, Repetition, and Eternal Recurrence," in *International Kierkegaard Commentary: Fear and Trembling and Repetition*, ed. Robert L. Perkins (Macon GA: Mercer University Press, 1993) 233n3, 244.

[14] Kierkegaard, *Repetition*, 203.

and significance of the other elements of his world because he has lost his primary object of concern, his beloved. He longs for a repetition; that is, he longs to see again the significance in himself and the world that he saw before losing his beloved,[15] to "have a double sense of [their] meaning."[16] Against all reasonable expectation, he predicts that such a repetition will occur after he has prepared himself to be a dutiful husband and so to marry his beloved. Surely then, he fondly imagines, she will return to him.

Eventually, the young man sends a letter asserting that he has finally experienced his repetition of meaning, though he has not experienced an external repetition as he had anticipated.[17] Of course, he is of dubious reliability as a narrator, and the reader may suspect that the young man has not completely grasped the concept of a repetition nor completely escaped self-deception.[18] Nevertheless, his story suggests the possibility of a genuine repetition, and, in the discourse's telling, Job seems to have experienced one. After all, his brief words end not in lament but in praise: "Blessed be the name of the Lord!" Surely only someone who had seen

---

[15] Ibid., 214–15.

[16] Ibid., 221. Alastair Hannay explains, "Repetition is 'repeating' or 'resuming' one's earlier experience from a higher vantage point, giving it a new, and deeper, unity." See *Kierkegaard: The Arguments of the Philosophers* (London: Routledge, 1991) 69.

[17] The gap between the young man's anticipated repetition and the repetition he claims actually to have experienced indicates that there are different kinds of repetitions. In a passage in his papers, Kierkegaard distinguishes three kinds of repetition roughly corresponding to the aesthetic, ethical, and religious life-views. For brief discussion and references, see Mooney, "*Repetition*," 303n11.

[18] Such suspicions increase when the reader learns that Kierkegaard altered the story from its original form to include the young man's self-proclaimed repetition, a repetition that occurs when he discovers that his beloved is marrying another man, only after he himself discovered that his lost love, Regine, was marrying. See Hannay, *Kierkegaard*, 346n52.

again the significance his world had lost could respond as Job does. Furthermore, since anyone may face a test like Job's, his example opens the possibility of repetition for all.[19] As a prototype, Job's life should encourage everyone to respond as he does. But such a task is no easy one, requiring nothing less than a transformation of character. Each one must acquire the virtues attributed to Job in the discourse, especially the virtues of gratitude, patience, and faith.

Only a spirit of thankfulness enabled Job to exclaim, in the midst of his losses, "The Lord gave and the Lord took away."[20] His thankfulness in this instance, no doubt, had a different character than the gratitude he expressed before his losses but was nevertheless equally honest. Because of his thankfulness, Job could recall the genuine beauty—neither lessened by regret nor increased by nostalgia—of what he had lost, the beauty that reflected the goodness of God, who gave the gifts to begin with.[21] Without this ability to remember the significance of what he had lost, Job could not have experienced a repetition, "a double sense of meaning." Similarly, his gratitude enabled him to relinquish his attachment to his losses, "as if it were not the Lord who took it away but Job who gave it back to him,"[22] since he saw them as gifts and not as achievements or entitlements. This relinquishment freed Job to see again the value of what he had lost, liberating him from a "nagging" fixation on his original sense of its meaning.[23]

But Job's gratitude did not imply a mere resignation to the vagaries of fate or a stoic refusal to credit the value of contingent goods. In the midst of his thankfulness, the

---

[19] Kierkegaard, *Eighteen Upbuilding Discourses*, 123–24.
[20] Ibid., 115–16.
[21] Ibid., 116.
[22] Ibid., 116–17.
[23] Ibid., 118.

discourse says, "he did not evade the thought that [everything] was lost."[24] But that thought failed to vitiate his thankfulness because "his soul remained quiet until the Lord's explanation again came to him and found his mind, like good earth, well cultivated in patience."[25] Patience is a "soul-strength"[26] that, paradoxically, makes one weak with respect to the things of the external world.[27] Patience holds the soul still and quiet, as it seeks to gain itself in relation to God through suffering in the external world.[28] Had Job not been patient, his suffering would soon have overwhelmed his thankfulness, and he would have lost his soul rather than gained it.

Job's patience and thankfulness both depended on his faith. By faith, Job saw God at work in his own suffering.[29] Rather than blaming his enemies or nature or even himself, Job simply confessed, "the Lord took away."[30] "Job traced everything back to God; he did not detain his soul and quench his spirit with deliberation or explanations that only feed and foster doubt, even though the person suspended in them does not even notice that."[31] But seeing God at work in one's suffering does not necessarily result in gratitude and patience; it may even work against such virtues. C. S. Lewis, for example, reflecting on the death of his wife, writes, "Not that I am (I think) in much danger of ceasing to believe in God. The real danger is of coming to believe such dreadful things about him. The conclusion I dread is not, 'So there's no God after all,' but, 'So this is what God's really like. Deceive yourself no

---

[24] Ibid.
[25] Ibid., 118–19.
[26] Ibid., 160.
[27] Ibid., 172
[28] Ibid., 171–72; cf. 116–19.
[29] Ibid., 121.
[30] Ibid., 119–20.
[31] Ibid., 121.

longer.'"[32] Job's faith, however, did not just see God but saw him as unconditionally good and as the source of every good. As a discourse published earlier in 1843 puts it, "he, the Father of lights, ever constant, at every moment makes everything good, makes everything a good and perfect gift for everyone who has enough heart to be humble, enough heart to be trustful. ...Every gift is a good and a perfect gift when it is received with thankfulness."[33] Or as the second of 1843's four discourses has it, "What, then, is the good? It is that which is from above."[34] In faith, Job saw what he had lost, and his losing it, in relation to the God who gives all and only good things.

Job's faith made his gratitude possible. Only one who sees God as the source of good and of nothing but good can give thanks to God when he loses his world. Job's patience sustained his faith by keeping his soul still and quiet, so that he did not lose his perception of God as the source of goodness. But at the same time, the reader might think that Job's patience depended on his faith, too, since in it he had a perception of God that made waiting for a repetition seem worthwhile.

Faith, gratitude, and patience make a repetition possible for the one who has suffered loss. Consequently, these four upbuilding discourses aim to encourage their reader to grow in those virtues. The second of the four, titled "Every Good and Every Perfect Gift Comes from Above," concerns the virtue of faith and the struggle with doubt. Gratitude and its complement, generosity, form the subject matter for the third, which repeats the previous title. The fourth ruminates on "gaining one's soul in patience." Though Job does not appear on stage in any of these last three discourses, his prompting

---

[32] C. S. Lewis, *A Grief Observed* (London: Faber and Faber Press, 1963; Rep. New York: Bantam, 1976) 5.

[33] Kierkegaard, *Eighteen Upbuilding Discourses*, 40–41.

[34] Ibid., 134.

sounds clearly in the background. For example, his conviction that God is the source of all and only good provides the object for faith and doubt in the second discourse and the shape of gratitude and generosity in the third. And his repetition provides the model for the growth in virtue presupposed by the other discourses. The rest of this chapter will explore the narrative pattern of repetition present in the third discourse's pedagogical strategies and the corresponding accounts of the emotions and of moral transitions.

Before moving to that exploration, note one last contextual feature. Besides Job's experience of repetition, his thankfulness, and his faith that God is the source of all and only good, yet another element structures the third discourse's meditations. As a corollary to the last conviction, the third discourse also insists on the equality of every person. Referring to the concept of divine goodness as captured in the title passage, the discourse asserts, "If that stands firm, then the difference is indeed canceled, because a difference in imperfection, which is indigenous in people's gifts, can only be transient, then at last the words of the apostle are continually heard as a divine refrain that is able to perfect every difference in equality before God."[35] Concepts of divine goodness and its corollary equality provide the context for the gratitude and generosity prized by the discourse. So the responsive reader moves, not from ingratitude to gratitude, but from one sense of giving's significance to another, more adequate one, shaped by genuinely religious concerns and concepts; and so as well for generosity. The responsive reader must, then, lose the first sense of giving and receiving's significance and meaning, so that he can see them again with eyes sharpened by the discourse's thoughts.

[35] Ibid., 145.

The Pedagogical Effects of Kierkegaard's Narratives

Arne Grøn argues that the characters described in the upbuilding discourses play "a methodological role" in Kierkegaard's attempt to depict virtues such as patience and courage as modes of resistance to the acids of temporality that threaten the human self.[36] Grøn rightly underscores the significance of Kierkegaard's use of characters and the importance of the passing of time for them. But Kierkegaard aims not merely to depict the virtues but to move his reader to acquire them. To that end, Kierkegaard configures the passing of time for his characters into a structured and repetitive set of narrative patterns. This section of the chapter describes the patterns of repetition that plot the third discourse's narratives.

The bulk of the discourse comprises thirteen brief narratives, each of which describes someone who moves from a lack of generosity or gratitude to the exemplification of one of those virtues. Written in the second person, these stories intend to bring "you the reader," as you see yourself in the characters, to lose your naïve grasp on the significance and value of giving and of giving thanks, and then to find a new perspective in which you see again their significance and value. This new sense, of course, is distinctively religious, shaped by genuinely religious concerns and concepts.

The discourse does not address the moral skeptic who needs to be convinced of the virtues' value. It assumes that, as someone "favorably disposed" to the discourse, you are already professedly committed to becoming religious,[37] but that you are also liable, in certain circumstances, to see giving

[36] "Temporality in Kierkegaard's Edifying Discourses," in *Kierkegaard Studies: Yearbook*, ed. Niels Jørgen Cappelørn, Hermann Dueser, and Jon Stewart (New York: Walter de Gruyter, 2000) 200–201. See also 195.

[37] Kierkegaard, *Eighteen Upbuilding Discourses*, 107.

and receiving in the light of concepts other than the essential truths found in the words of the Apostle James and repeated in the discourse's title. Even worse, you tend to conceal from yourself the tenuousness of your virtues, preferring to think of yourself as morally mature. Consequently, the discourse sets you in circumstances that disclose the limits of your ability to see giving generously and receiving gratefully as of central significance for you. Those disorienting circumstances reveal that you actually see the significance of giving and receiving only in relation to concepts and concerns that fail to exhibit religious earnestness. But they also provide an opportunity for the discourse to reshape your perception in distinctively religious ways. After you grasp more adequately the religious concepts that the discourse uncovers, and connect them to your concern for becoming religious, you may learn to see giving and receiving anew. You may finally come to see them in a religiously authentic way. Three examples of this pattern follow.

Imagine yourself first as a *joyless giver*.[38] In this character, you see the significance of giving in terms of its effectiveness at meeting the manifest needs of another, especially for that which will ensure the equality of all. Giving's value follows from its place in a kind of hypothetical imperative: if this need is to be met, you must make the gift that will meet it. Since, as the "favorably disposed" person you are,[39] you are committed to the value of meeting others' needs, you can easily see that you should make this gift. So you are willing to give, but you find no joy in the giving, any more than you would find joy in the calorie counting necessary for your desired weight loss. But you can, of course, easily imagine circumstances in which

[38] Ibid., 145–46.

[39] Ibid., 107.

giving would lose even the significance your present perspective assigns it and in which, consequently, you would find yourself immobilized, not readily able to act decisively in a giving manner. For instance, if you could imagine that anyone else might make the gift that meets the need, you would find it difficult to decide to give yourself. Circumstances like those, then, loosen your grasp on the significance of giving. But the discourse loosens your grasp in another way as well. Since all good things are from God and human equality before God depends on that truth, the discourse points out, your gift is always unnecessary and never sufficient for achieving the equality at which it aims. With those truths fixed in your mind, you may find it difficult to recognize the same sort of significance that you saw before in any kind of giving. Your grasp on giving, then, is deficient in two ways: it cannot be counted on in a wide variety of circumstances and, even when you do give, it lacks the affect of joy that should accompany it.

But the discourse's story raises new hopes. If you can lose that sense of giving's significance, perhaps you can recover another. Since giving depends on the divine goodness, perhaps you can begin to see giving's significance now in the way that it puts you and the receiver together, equally, before God. In a later passage, the discourse describes how giving admonition to another (as the discourse does to the reader), enacting a kind of repetition, can make the admonition "as fresh and vivid in your soul as it was in the moment of acquisition."[40] Perhaps in this story, in the character of the joyless giver, you hope that the significance of giving can again become fresh and vivid, even if different from your naïve perspective. But the discourse disappoints this hope. Almost accusingly, the discourse

[40] Ibid., 149.

declares, "But you learned another kind of wisdom, that there is no good gift either up there or down here, and you could just as well keep everything or give everything away."[41] Seeing yourself in the story's mirror, you can imagine how such circumstances might take away your perception of giving's significance, since it would no longer demonstrate your ability to bring about equality for others (itself a perception that subtly undermines genuine equality). You continue to read, hoping to find in the story a new way of seeing giving in such circumstances. But no repetition is forthcoming; turning dizzily in the darkness from heaven to earth, you fail to see again the significance of giving. You have learned the aesthete's version of wisdom, a wisdom that makes true choice impossible: whether you give or do not give, you will regret it either way.[42]

Nevertheless, as the reader you are not bound by the perceptions of the characters in the discourse's story. The significance of the story, according to the preface of *Four Upbuilding Discourses*, finally lies not in its own narrative world but in its repetition in the reader's life. Your appropriate reception of the story "sanctifies the gift, gives it meaning, and transforms it into much."[43] Just as you could not predict the conclusion of the story as the discourse tells it, neither can you predict with certainty the prospects for the story's repetition in your own. But by turning your reflection against you through the story, the discourse has at least made possible the loss that must precede the repetition.

Imagine yourself next as a bitter, *reluctant giver*.[44] As this character, you see someone facing a problem or circumstance relevantly similar to one you yourself have faced at some

---

[41] Ibid., 146.

[42] Kierkegaard, *Either/Or*, 1:38–39.

[43] Kierkegaard, *Eighteen Upbuilding Discourses*, 107.

[44] Ibid., 149–50.

earlier time. You recall that, after much bitter struggle, you overcame the adversity, and you recognize that you are now in a place to help others by passing along what wisdom you have gained. So you see a significance to giving in these circumstances—your gift will produce equality between you and another by transferring your hard-won advantage to that other. At the same time, your grip on that significance is quickly failing, and your circumstances have all but robbed you of it. You, after all, won this wisdom the hard way, and you set a high value on it accordingly. You consider, then, that it might be better to make this one who needs such wisdom also pay for it in the bitterness of struggle, before receiving your advice. Perhaps that person will then value it as highly as you do.

So this scenario takes you, as the "favorably disposed" reader, from a willingness to give to circumstances in which, in the story's mirror, you lose completely your grasp of the positive significance of giving. But your loss proves that your perception was, in the first instance, naïve at best. If the bitterness of your struggle compared with the potential ease of the receiver could cloud your vision, then you must have seen the source of the gift's goodness in your effort in the struggle. And though you were willing to give so as to effect equality between you and the receiver, you had in mind only a certain kind of equality. You wished for an equality in achievement, and the gratuitousness of your gift threatens that possibility. So that perception of giving's significance cannot provide for reliability in giving or enable giving free from bitterness and reluctance. The reluctant giver is also joyless.

The discourse's guiding words—every good and every perfect gift comes from above—shape a different perception. Seen in their light, the gift of admonition has its value not in view of its relation to the bitter experience that produced its wisdom but in light of God's goodness and ability to make it fruitful in the life of another. Since you cannot know what God and the other will make of it, the discourse insists that you see yourself as more insignificant than your gift. The goodness of the gift comes from God, not the giver's effort. And consequently, the gift makes possible an equality before God, relegating differences in achievement to the inessential.

The discourse opens the possibility, then, of gaining back your sense of giving's significance, this time in a form more impervious to the threats of changing circumstances. But once again, the discourse does not neatly answer expectation. Rather than provide the ending to the story, the discourse provides words of advice: "If, then, you do have an admonition to give, do not lift your head high in censure, do not open your eyes to probe, but bow your head and your eyes under the admonition so that it may sound from above just as meaningfully for you as for the other."[45] As you follow that advice in imagination, the story suggests the possibility of a repetition. But the discourse refuses to provide a definitive resolution, just as it refuses to predict your reception of its gift of itself. Whether you, as the reader, will experience your own repetition is something neither story nor discourse nor, perhaps, even you can declare with certainty.

Imagine yourself, finally, as a *dominated receiver,* obliged to accept a gift from a rich and powerful person.[46] This powerful person disregards you, "since the whole affair was trifling and meaningless to him."[47] The giver sees himself as so superior to you that he sees value in neither the gift nor the thanks. He is

---

[45] Ibid., 150.
[46] Ibid., 153–55.
[47] Ibid., 154.

like Aristotle's magnanimous man, who, "if he is honored by just anyone, or for something small,...will entirely disdain it."[48] You, however, are to see yourself not as the magnanimous man, but as the lowly one who seeks to thank him for some boon, vital to you but inconsequential to him. Looking at yourself as you appear in the magnanimous man's eyes, you see that you harm yourself by expressing thanks, since that act confirms your inequality.[49] Perhaps you can already feel your sense of the significance of giving thanks slipping away, and resentment boiling to the surface. In such circumstances, you may easily lose your grip on the significance of thanking your benefactor, since such acts seem to make you complicit in your own domination by another.

The discourse ruthlessly takes from you your sense of thanksgiving's significance—but only because its naivety makes it unreliable and embittering. Your naïve perspective sees the magnanimous man as he himself does, as the source of the goodness of the gift. Consequently, giving thanks has meaning only in relation to him. Furthermore, you desire equality with him, but only the kind of equality he can recognize and respect. His calloused disregard of you and your thanks makes achieving that impossible. But when the Apostle James's words shape your perception, you see the same story in a different way, so that you can see again the significance of giving thanks in relation to God's goodness and the corollary human equality.[50]

---

[48] Aristotle, *Nicomachean Ethics*_(1124a10–11), trans. Terence Irwin (Indianapolis IN: Hackett Publishing Company, 1985) 100.

[49] Kierkegaard, *Eighteen Upbuilding Discourses*, 153–54.

[50] When you give thanks to the magnanimous man in light of your new concept of gratitude, he may not recognize your words or actions as gratitude, since they will not credit him as the final source of the goodness of his gift. In his papers, Kierkegaard asserts that if you love your neighbors in the Christian sense, "you must be able to bear that your love for them is regarded as hate"

According to the discourse, "The lowly man is served by the powerful, and in your thanksgiving you lifted your heart up to God for having used that powerful man as an instrument to help you."[51] Now you see that the gift reveals not an inequality between you and the magnanimous man but a common dependence on God. He, even if unknowingly, expresses his dependence on God through giving, and you through thanking, and together you are united in a common confession that each is "*more insignificant than the gift*."[52]

Like the other two, this little story exemplifies the kind of repetition suggested in the narratives of Job and *Repetition's* Young Man. In each case, the reader can discern at least four possible moments. First, the stories present the central characters as attached to some finite object of concern that provides them with a first, naïve sense of the value and significance of their world. Next, some external event or circumstance causes them to lose their grasp on the object of concern. After that, they become unable to maintain their naïve vision of the significance of themselves, their activities, their surroundings, and so on. That inability renders them immobile and despairing. Finally, in the moment most properly termed a repetition, they may gain a new vision of their world, seeing it anew in the light of a more adequate object of concern and finding a more reliable and appropriate sense of its significance.

(quoted in Søren Kierkegaard, *Works of Love*, ed. and trans. Howard V. Hong and Edna H. Hong [Princeton NJ: Princeton University Press, 1995] 441). Similarly, gratitude repeated might not look like gratitude at all to those who, like the magnanimous man, have never suffered the loss of their naïve perception. I owe the formulation of this point to a conversation with Robert E. Colton.

[51] Kierkegaard, *Eighteen Upbuilding Discourses*, 154.

[52] Ibid., 156–57.

These moments vary in their intensity, length, and depth. The Young Man's experience of the third moment—the loss of his beloved and the consequent loss of significance in his world—is of much greater duration and force than the corresponding experience for Job. In fact, Job moves so quickly from loss to repetition that the blindness to significance the Young Man suffers seems almost a mere possibility in his story. The Young Man's repetition, on the other hand, seems shallower than Job's; one wonders if the Young Man's experience should even count as a repetition rather than an instance of self-deception.

In another contrast, some of the characters in "Every Good and Every Perfect Gift" find their way to a repetition and some do not. The joyless giver, for example, does not, while the reluctant giver's fate is left ambiguous. Only the dominated receiver experiences a true repetition. But despite the diversity of these stories' endings, their plots follow a similar narrative pattern that Kierkegaard captures under the rubric of a repetition.

Because the discourse addresses itself primarily to the "favorably disposed" reader, one might expect that it would deploy characters with fundamentally religious concerns. But if one pays careful attention, one can see that these characters are not concerned most of all with their relation to God, though they seem to have convinced themselves that they are. Since these stories are mirrors for the reader, as you read them they aim to uncover your hidden concerns as well. You may take Kierkegaard's reference to the "favorably disposed" reader as a congratulating pat on the back, acknowledging your own maturity. But as you see yourself in the stories of the discourse, that pat becomes a different kind of blow all together, knocking your moral self-complacency from you. As the joyless giver, for example, you are most concerned not with your relation to God but with your unique ability to bring about equality for others through your own efforts and, perhaps, with others' recognition of that ability. Consequently, circumstances that reveal you as unnecessary for the equality of others take from you that object of concern and cause you to lose sight of the significance of giving generously. Similarly, as the reluctant giver, your concern is for your status as a self-made individual. Circumstances that suggest the triviality of that status threaten your sense of giving's significance. As the dominated receiver, your concern is for others' recognition of your equal status and worth. The callous attitudes of the dominating giver cause you to lose your perception of the significance of giving thanks.

In all these stories, adverse circumstances reveal your concerns as not genuinely religious and as fixed instead on finite, external objects. Those inadequate concerns distort your perceptions of giving generously and receiving gratefully, rendering you incapable of acting virtuously. But in the last example, that of the dominated receiver, the discourse shows the difference made by cultivating a concern for one's relation to God and understanding that concern under properly formed concepts. Taking your relation to God as your central concern and understanding God as the source of goodness and the guarantor of human equality reshape your perception of the significance of giving thanks even in the most difficult of circumstances.

Emotions and Kierkegaard's Narrative Pedagogy

Imagine yourself again as the joyless giver. In this story, your naïve sense of giving's significance makes it nothing more than a means to an end separate from itself. Considered apart from its utility in bringing about the equality you desire, it has no particular positive significance for you, constituting instead a mere drain on your resources. Even considered as a means to your desired end, giving is necessary but not particularly desirable. To the extent that you experience joy, you experience it merely in the outcome, not in the act of giving itself. But if you developed a concern for God as the source of goodness and saw the significance of giving in light of your relation to him, the act of giving itself would have a deep and positive meaning and would be a source of joy for you. Your joylessness, then, suggests that your perceptions are faulty and that you have failed to internalize the truths of the text the discourse expounds. You have not grasped the true import of these acts of generosity or gratitude. Imagine yourself as the reluctant giver or as the dominated receiver and you can trace the same pattern. Your emotions change with your perceptions and indicate the extent to which you have internalized the truths about divine goodness and human equality at the center of the discourse. Explaining the pedagogical effects of the discourse's narratives, then, depends on an account of the emotions that weaves tightly together their perceptual quality and their intimate relations to concepts and concerns.

In "Existence, Emotion, and Virtue: Classical Themes in Kierkegaard," Robert C. Roberts clarifies Kierkegaard's understanding of the emotions. His remarks can explain the assumptions about the emotions and their moral significance on which the discourse's narrative pedagogy depends. According to Roberts, Kierkegaard holds that emotions are based on concerns, shaped by thoughts, and experienced as perceptions. A concern is an interest, passion, or attachment of a person that provides the ground for a range of emotions. Roberts uses the example of someone who owns a small business that is the object of her chief concern. She is likely to feel joy when business is going well, pride when her products and services are excellent, and so on. Her emotional responses depend on her interest in her business. Thoughts play their role, too, however. Though Kierkegaard does not simply identify emotions with thoughts, he does insist that the ways in which we conceptualize the objects of our emotions shape them into the kinds of emotions they are. Roberts writes, "In his upbuilding discourses Kierkegaard repeatedly instructs us on how to *think* so as to have, or not to have, a given emotion."[53]

Certainly, in this discourse, Kierkegaard spends much of his energy on the concepts that underlie correct or incorrect moral perceptions. But his repeated use of perceptual metaphors also suggests another point. Roberts writes, "While emotions are shaped by thoughts, the fact that they focus specific kinds of features of the situations they are about, and do so in terms of the concerns on which they are based, makes them as much like perceptions as like *mere* thoughts."[54] Emotional responses, then, are "a kind of immediate impression of the way things are (the way God is, the way oneself is, the way the world is), the most natural metaphor for which is sense perception."[55] Anger, for instance, may be a perception of someone's action toward oneself as an undeserved slight to one's dignity. In that case, it is also a perception of the importance of one's dignity for oneself. And as Roberts argues, one's being struck in that way clearly depends on one's concern for one's own dignity and on a

[53] Robert C. Roberts, "Existence, Emotion, and Virtue," in *The Cambridge Companion to Kierkegaard*, ed. Alastair Hannay and Gordon Marino (New York: Cambridge University Press, 1998) 190. For a fuller description of the emotions and their moral significance, see his *Emotions: An Essay in Aid of Moral Psychology* (New York: Cambridge University Press, 2003).

[54] Roberts, "Existence, Emotion, and Virtue," 195–96.

[55] Ibid., 197.

concept of that dignity that specifies what counts as a slight to it.

This account of the emotions renders the discourse's pedagogical strategy both intelligible in its narrative form and promising in its pedagogical effects.[56] As already noted, the preface to *Four Upbuilding Discourses* declares that the reader who can receive the discourses meaningfully is one who is "favorably disposed."[57] The discourse's strategy assumes the reader's professed concern for becoming religious, though it also reveals opposing concerns hidden in the reader's own inner being. Consequently, the discourse assumes that it has no need to convince the reader that he or she ought to love his or her neighbor or to give generously or to receive with thankfulness or even to value human equality. If you imagine yourself in the discourse's stories as being without these concerns and their attendant construals, then you will surely miss their drama.

So the discourse focuses on the concepts of divine goodness and its corollary human equality. It shows that a naïve perception of giving or receiving's significance often results from false or inadequate conceptualizations of central objects of concern. The discourse uncovers them by putting the reader into circumstances in which certain conceptualizations

---

[56] If my focus were not on the narrative character of Kierkegaard's pedagogy, I might also take the time to argue that a narrative form, in turn, renders many, if not all, emotions intelligible. One could begin by noting that certain emotions, such as anger or jealousy, bring with them not just a simple construal but one that includes a task; we see the situation in terms of something to be done, an action to be undertaken that is characteristic of those experiencing this emotion. Further, insofar as every emotion is constituted by concerns, the gift and task structure is general to them all, since the concerns reflect one's actuality and typically call for some kind of response. Combining these claims with the connection between narrative and the gift and task structure outlined in my first chapter would, I think, bring this point home.

[57] Kierkegaard, *Eighteen Upbuilding Discourses*, 107.

of God's relation to humans cannot sustain a perception of the value of giving generously or receiving gratefully for the reader. In this way, it opens the possibility of a repetition that enables the reader to see their significance again, but this time in a more adequate and stable way.

If emotions are modes of perception, then this repetition may appear as a shift in emotional responses. The characters' new vision is not a mere matter of reflective cognition, but more a matter of an immediate perception-like grasp, as they begin, in the best scenarios, to give gladly rather than grudgingly or to receive joyfully rather than reluctantly. For the reader, reflecting in a concerned way on the discourse's imagined narratives promotes this kind of moral seeing.

If emotions are based on concerns and shaped by thought, then a change in one's concerns and thoughts may alter one's emotional responses. But one cannot change one's emotions just by deciding to change one's thoughts. Emotions have a perceptual aspect, and perceptual transitions cannot, at least normally, be directly willed. After all, the discourse does not always present stories that end as the reader hopes, nor does it even claim knowledge of the resolution for every story. Moral transitions, such as the ones the discourse describes, are not the inevitable result of effort, but gifts for which one waits in patience and faith and gratitude. Like gifts, they are not necessary, but neither are they arbitrary.

Developmental Models

I have argued so far that the discourse deploys its pedagogical narratives with the aim of sparking a perceptual transition, necessarily involving the emotions, as a moment in the task of becoming virtuous, religiously understood. But nothing about Kierkegaard's pedagogical strategy compels his reader from one kind of perception to another. There is no causal force, no psychological conditioning with a necessary, Skinnerian result. Nor is there a deductive move from one perception to another, no syllogism, the necessary conclusion of which is the new perception. As examples of repetitions, the recovery of what was lost, the transitions to more complete virtue depicted in the discourse cannot be forced. *Repetition*'s Young Man and the discourses' Job must simply wait for a storm that gives their worlds and themselves back to them. So the transition is contingent. What kind of model captures the notion of moral development the discourses imply, if we discard the analogy of a deductive syllogism or forcible conditioning?

Organic growth provides an intuitively appealing image. A plant's growth to maturity—a seed, fallen from the plant and buried in the ground, develops its potential through stages of growth, and finally brings forth new life and new seeds—suggests several of the aspects of moral development already discussed. The plant's life moves from less adequate to more adequate stages of functioning as it responds to its environment, just as a person moves from less to more adequate moral stages in response to the moral and social environment. Even the seed's burial in the ground could represent the loss of meaning that precedes a repetition. Its environment introduces an element of contingency, so that no one can predict with certainty whether this seedling will move successfully through its stages of maturity or not. Thus organic growth depicts a movement through stages that a deductive syllogism obscures, but at the same time suggests also a principle of reasonable explanation for growth or its absence. When we talk about moral growth or cultivating our souls, or even the concept of development itself, some such set of analogies must be in play.

But the organic model proves inadequate in at least two ways. First, it fails to capture the right kind of contingency. A normal seed might or might not grow to maturity because its environmental conditions might or might not prove conducive. And with the right knowledge and the right tools, with the ability to manipulate a seed's external conditions as necessary, one could be pretty confident that one could cause the seed to grow as one wished. But the contingency built into moral transitions is not of this kind. There is no knowledge, no tool, and no skill that can make moral transitions as predictable as hydroponic gardening. Their contingency extends even beyond the unpredictability of a particular human's choosing, for they do not follow necessarily even when willed. Like a perceptual gestalt shift, they sometimes take place suddenly after much desire and a long wait.

This contingency raises the specter of arbitrariness. If the transition does not have to go the way it does, then why is one kind of transition better than another or better than none at all? After all, a syllogistic or organically causal connection gives one assurance that the next move is the right one. But without any such connection, how can one be sure which next move is the right one? The narrative strategies of the third discourse's pedagogy suggest an answer.

We may take a cue here from Aristotle's discussion of tragic narrative in the *Poetics*. Aristotle argues that a tragic narrative represents one complete action and that the incidents that make it up "have the greatest effect on the mind when they occur unexpectedly and at the same time in consequence of one another."[58] On this account, successful narratives have an aspect of contingency in that one cannot predict their

[58] Aristotle, *Poetics* (1452a1–4), trans. Ingram Bywater, in *The Basic Works of Aristotle*, ed. Richard McKeon (New York: Random House, 1941) 1465.

transitions, but they are nevertheless non-arbitrary, since the incidents occur "in consequence of one another." Aristotle attributes these features to tragic narrative specifically, but a little reflection on our own experience with stories reveals that the surprising but fitting connection between events is characteristic of stories in any genre. What stories require for unity and non-arbitrariness, then, is not a necessary, predictable connection between incidents. Instead, their unity lies in connections discernible in retrospect as fitting. The moments of the narrative follow one another in an appropriate way, even if one could not have predicted their sequence before the narrative unfolded.[59]

But if this is true of stories, then Kierkegaard's narrative pedagogy assumes that it is also true of moral transitions, since it presents them in narrative form. If "rational" means "effected by syllogistic deliberation" or "explainable by cause and effect relations," as in a plant's growth, then such transitions will be non-rational. But being non-rational in that sense does not entail any sort of vicious arbitrariness or irrationality.[60] Instead, the moral transition the discourse works to bring about will be entirely reasonable if it can be seen to fit with what came before from a retrospective point of view. The discourse supplies the means to see that fittingness when it offers the conceptual clarification that allows the characters to see again the significance of activities whose value had been obscured by the loss of central objects of concern. That clarification follows on a kind of unmasking, in which it reveals the ways in which you as the reader, seeing yourself in

[59] See Kierkegaard, *Two Ages*, 35.

[60] For a similar argument, see John McDowell, "Might There Be External Reasons?" in *Mind, Value, and Reality* (Cambridge MA: Harvard University Press, 1998) 107.

the mirror of a character's story, have worked to keep authentically religious concepts and concerns from shaping your vision. As the reluctant giver, for instance, your attachment to your own sufferings as proof of your wisdom and courage makes you seem peculiarly significant, in a way that has its appeal to your pride, even if it makes it impossible to sustain generosity in the circumstances the discourse's story depicts. Furthermore, you can explain why you were formerly satisfied with your naïve perception, by referring to the concerns and concepts Kierkegaard's pedagogy uncovers. Finally, you can explain the fittingness of the denouement as a recovery, in a fuller and more adequate form, of what you lost through the accidents of changing circumstances. Your account of your moral transition, then, will be autobiographical and not strictly syllogistic or available from a third-person perspective as in a description of organic growth.[61] And, thus, it will be no more arbitrary than any other autobiography.[62]

An organic model also fails because it explains moral growth chiefly by reference to the capacities latent in the seed.[63] Everything required for the maturity of the plant, apart from external environmental factors, is present in the seed. Given

---

[61] See Charles Taylor's *Sources of the Self: The Making of Modern Identity* (Cambridge MA: Harvard University Press, 1989), especially pages 62–75, for further argument along these lines.

[62] Of course, some autobiographies are quite arbitrary, and perhaps all are to some degree. The discourse's pedagogical strategy offers some defenses against such arbitrariness in its unmasking of base motives, in its dialogical method (which requires you, the reader, to take account of another's interpretation of your own life), and in its bringing you, the reader, to awareness of your God-relation (which provides the final, inescapable context for the truth and intelligibility of judgments on life-stories, since God is the source of all and only good).

[63] Compare Judge William in Kierkegaard, *Either/Or*, 2:225: "From this you see what esthetic development signifies; it is a development just like that of a plant, and although the individual becomes, he becomes that which he immediately is."

the right environment and coaxing, those latent capacities naturally unfold into a mature plant, as it fulfills its essential possibilities. But consider, for example, the peculiar character of faith, gratitude, and patience, the virtues that prepare Job for his repetition. They are less fulfilling than emptying of the person they characterize, as the following claims from the *Four Upbuilding Discourses* demonstrate. The call to *patience* will "always come inopportunely, capable of simultaneously killing every bold expectancy that longs for renowned deeds, for inspired achievements,"[64] insisting that "a person can truly possess the imperfect only by surrendering it."[65] The person who receives *gratefully* "confesses that *he is more insignificant than the gift*,"[66] voiding his or her own claims to independent meaning and abandoning himself or herself to another. *Faith* requires renouncing demonstration and dying to the doubt that makes one strive for it.[67] A discourse published in 1844, titled "To Need God Is a Human Being's Highest Perfection," even goes so far as to claim that "the highest [power of a human being] is this: that a person is fully convinced that he himself is capable of nothing, nothing at all."[68] One struggles for one's own "annihilation," since "the annihilation is his truth."[69]

These sentences are hard sayings, undoubtedly meant to provoke, and apparently departing from concepts such as health and flourishing that are at home in an organic context. Becoming religious, they insist, means not to achieve but to receive. They present gratitude as central because the condition

---

[64] Kierkegaard, *Eighteen Upbuilding Discourses*, 159.
[65] Ibid., 165.
[66] Ibid., 156–57.
[67] Ibid., 135.
[68] Ibid., 307.
[69] Ibid., 309.

for a repetition lies not in the individual but in God. The recovery of meaning and the acquisition of virtues are finally gifts from another. A model of moral development that overlooks this fact overlooks the exemplarity of Job, and will make it very difficult to bring alive in the individual essentially religious ideas like those of the Apostle James.

In this respect, even a narrative model of development has its dangers. If one thinks of the retrospective fittingness of events in a narrative as analogous to the way in which God's gifts meet needs one never fully understands one has until one receives the gift, then one may remain close to the spirit of the religious discourses. But if one thinks, as seems reasonable, that the retrospective fittingness of events in a well-constructed narrative is obvious because those events fulfill some tension, some foreshadowing, initially overlooked in the preceding events of the story, then the essentially religious point becomes lost. Instead of directing attention to one's God-relation, such a narrative model focuses one's sight on one's own capacities. So, as an analogue for moral development, that feature of narrative intelligibility may suggest what the organic model suggests: that becoming virtuous fulfills some positive capacity latent in the individual. Timothy Jackson identifies this kind of doctrine as "Pelagianism": "the doctrine that we can have faith and earn salvation by means of our own intrinsic resources; human nature is perfectible, and no special grace is required."[70] Jackson argues convincingly that Kierkegaard rejects any version of Pelagianism throughout his religious writings. What model, then, can capture the sense of non-arbitrary contingency found in narratives but without losing the

---

[70] Timothy P. Jackson, "Arminian Edification: Kierkegaard on Grace and Free Will," in *The Cambridge Companion to Kierkegaard*, ed. Alastair Hannay and Gordon D. Marino (Cambridge: Cambridge University Press, 1998) 236.

religious spirit? The limitations of the present project do not allow a full answer to the question, but a suggestion will emerge in the fifth chapter, in a discussion of Kierkegaard's own sense of the limits of narrative.

Conclusion

The *Four Upbuilding Discourses* of 1843 present a connected series of meditations meant to aid the reader in acquiring the faith, gratitude, and patience exemplified by Job. His benediction, the keynote for his paradigmatic life, expresses a repetition. After the loss of his most central objects of concern, Job's faith, patience, and gratitude enable him to see again the meaning and significance of his world. Each of the other discourses attempts to cultivate in the reader one of those virtues, so that the reader's own story can also have the character of a repetition. Cultivating those virtues requires a transformation of moral perception, consisting in a renewed pattern of emotional responses, and received as a gift, a transformation that calls for narrative display. *Works of Love* develops these themes, telling the story of the implied reader's reception of the gift of Christian love, i.e., the transformation of his moral perception in the light of God's command and Christ's mission. The next chapter takes up that narrative.

4

Love and Authority in *Works of Love*'s Pedagogical Narrative

The Implied Narrative of Repetition in *Works of Love*

In chapter 2, I briefly described the implied reader of *Works of Love* and sketched the plot of a narrative of repetition embedded in the text that features the implied reader as a primary character. This chapter focuses more closely on Kierkegaard's story of the implied reader's education into neighbor love, as the reader moves from the confusions of Christendom to the works of love. After identifying the narrative pattern of repetition in *Works of Love* and its pedagogical aims, I begin by describing the implied reader as a character, focusing on three central traits that characterize him[1] at various stages of his story and that provide the key to its organization. Next, I describe the role of authority in a formation in Christian love. Finally, I argue that Christian love is a unique virtue, contextualizing all the others, and thus making a repetition possible.

[1] I have found no satisfactory way to avoid a gendered pronoun in reference to the implied reader. Plural forms suggest more than one implied reader, which would confuse the issue, and Kierkegaard's text in *Works of Love* does not facilitate the use of the second person as it does in *Eighteen Upbuilding Discourses*. Because the implied reader is the same character throughout the narrative, shifting from one gender to the other poses problems of its own. I have chosen the masculine form because Kierkegaard himself surely thought in those terms, but I hope all my readers, whether male or female, may find themselves in the story.

The Narrative Pattern of Repetition in Works of Love *and Its Pedagogical Aims.* *Works of Love* is best known for its violent attacks on such preferential loves as friendship and romantic relationships. Not infrequently, defenders of Kierkegaard argue that his harsh claims about preferential love are meant only to "dethrone" it and not to abolish it. This claim is correct as far as it goes. But it fails to discern a deeper structure in Kierkegaard's deliberations, reducing them to mere argument. Too often his harshness then becomes simply a matter of exaggerated rhetoric that must be mitigated or explained away to get at his more acceptable points. But reflection on the implied reader's narrative reveals a pattern of repetition deeply embedded in the first series of deliberations that can point to a more adequate reading of the text.[2]

The narrative moves through the following stages. The implied reader first identifies preferential love as preferential, clarifying his naïve perception of love's significance. Then he loses preferential love in his confrontation with the divine command to love one's neighbor.[3] Finally, after reorientation to Christianity's task and joy,[4] he finds himself seeing in a new way the meaning of what he had lost. His new vision recontextualizes and returns the preferential love he had earlier lost, but now focuses its significance in new terms. This pattern of repetition explains the harshness of the rhetoric without explaining it away. The early deliberations must cause the implied reader to lose his naïve perceptions if he is to gain a more adequate perspective, and the rhetoric is precisely and

[2] See ch. 2 for a brief overview of this narrative pattern in *Works of Love*.

[3] That this loss is disorienting in the way ch. 2 describes can easily be seen in those commentators who take that loss as a static claim about the nature of love, rather than a moment in a larger narrative. Such critics find *Works of Love* an inhuman work, because it seems to rob every human relation of significance.

[4] Kierkegaard, *Works of Love*, 62–64.

appropriately calibrated for that purpose. Even the early sections do not constitute an intemperate screed for the sake of shock.

A passage in the second deliberation lays out the pattern of repetition, as it clarifies the distinction between Christian love and preferential love. It is worth quoting at length. Kierkegaard writes,

> Take a pagan who is not spoiled by having learned thoughtlessly to patter Christianity by rote or has not been spoiled by the delusion of being a Christian—and this commandment, "You *shall* love," will not only surprise him but will disturb him, will be an offense to him. For this very reason that which is the mark of Christianity—"Everything has become new"—again fits the commandment of love. The commandment is not something new in an accidental sense, nor a novelty in the sense of something curious, nor something new in a temporal sense. Love had existed also in paganism, but this obligation to love is a change of eternity—and everything has become new.[5]

The marks of repetition all occur here. The pagan loses his initial love through a collision with the commandment, but then receives again what he had lost as everything becomes new, including love. Kierkegaard goes further, distinguishing between several senses of "new." The newness that comes through a repetition is not accidental, the mere addition of a new but inessential property to an old thing, like a new coat of paint on an old junker. It is not a novelty that presents a new moment of aesthetic experience and then becomes old in its turn. It is not new in a temporal sense, as if the old love belonged to a preceding moment left behind in the journey of time and the new love belongs to the next, passing moment.

---

[5] Ibid., 25. The internal quote is from 2 Corinthians 5:17.

Instead it is "a change of eternity," a qualitative change, a change in one's whole world of meaning. This new love has the permanence of eternity. It also has eternity's relation to time. Because eternity is equally related to each moment of time, the newness of its love is always constant and never grows old. Kierkegaard's task is, in a way, to make the implied reader a pagan, so that he can perceive the authentic newness of Christian love. In other words, he must make the implied Christian reader aware of the offense of the law in the way that the pagan would naturally be. To that end he makes the implied reader a character in a narrative that recapitulates the experience of the pagan's learning to love.

A key to this reading appears towards the end of the last deliberation in the first series. There Kierkegaard gives the hints that make a retrospective interpretation of the implied reader's narrative possible. He describes the pagan's learning experience by distinguishing between the kinds of collisions that might produce unhappy love. Before Christianity, he argues, people recognized the possibility that love's conflict with its circumstances or with different understandings of love might negate it. But "the world before the time of Christianity never saw that in loving there was the possibility of a collision between two conceptions between which there was a difference of eternity, between the divine conception and the merely human conception."[6] This collision causes the offense for the pagan, an offense that loosens his grasp on his prior understanding of his loves and their objects. Without the collision, there could be no offense; without the offense, no loss; without the loss, no repetition, no recovery of love in a

---

[6] Kierkegaard, *Works of Love*, 109.

new and more adequate context. So *Works of Love* sets about to cause that offense, since every Christian is first a pagan.[7]

One such passage uses the conventions of a fairy tale to explain the circumstances and aims of *Works of Love*.

> If Christianity is to be preached out of the enchantment of illusion and deformed transmogrification (alas, it is like the fairy tale about the castle enchanted for a hundred years), then first of all the possibility of offense must be thoroughly preached back to life again. Only the possibility of offense (the antidote to the sleeping potion of apologetics) is able to rouse the one who has fallen asleep, is able to revoke the enchantment so that Christianity is itself again. ...Truly, if Christianity will just again rise up formidable with the possibility of offense so this horror can again startle people—then Christianity will need no defense.[8]

Here, at the end of the first series of deliberations, Kierkegaard provides another clue for reading the entire series, and his use of fairy-tale conventions gives it a narrative cast. He suggests a fairy tale with a setting, an exposition, a task, and a possible denouement. The setting, of course, is the castle, a lofty, impregnable fortress, self-sufficient and seemingly independent. The castle represents Christendom, smug in its self-congratulation and the context for Kierkegaard's own authorship, including *Works of Love*. The exposition, were it explicit, would describe how the inhabitants of this seemingly impregnable castle fell under the influence of an evil enchantment that makes them sleepwalk through their lives, unaware of the true significance of their actions and disengaged from their movements. But Kierkegaard does not

---

[7] Ibid., 26.

[8] Ibid., 200. See also the surrounding pages and the supplement on p. 446.

provide all those details here, merely stating that the castle inhabitants find themselves already enchanted. Similarly, though Kierkegaard elsewhere meditates on the origins of Christendom's existential sleepiness (for example, in the discussion of original sin in *The Concept of Anxiety*; the description of the stages and forms of despair in *Either/Or* and *The Sickness Unto Death*; and the social analysis of *Two Ages*), in *Works of Love* he mostly takes its presence for granted.[9] He identifies the magical potion as "apologetics," by which he means, "speaking ingratiatingly about the essentially Christian."[10] To practice apologetics, in this sense, is to urge others to take up Christianity and its "two-edged" sword as if they were "a bouquet of flowers."[11] Overcoming the power of this enchantment by delivering to its victims the antidote constitutes the task in the story. And, of course, the antidote is the possibility of offense that makes a repetition possible.

The fairy tale this passage suggests captures *Works of Love*'s implied narrative, with the implied author delivering the antidote and the implied reader moving from enchantment to freedom.[12] Though the hero of the fairy tale may remain hidden from view, the implied author reveals himself in the telling of the story. Likewise, one can infer the qualities of the implied reader from the larger narrative of the work as a whole, even though the inhabitants of the enchanted castle do not appear in any detail. Detailing these habits, as I do in the

[9] But not entirely. See, for example, Kierkegaard, *Works of Love*, 80 and 128, passages that anticipate Nietszche's analysis of *ressentiment* as the origin of a transvaluation of values.

[10] Kierkegaard, *Works of Love*, 198.

[11] Ibid. See also Heb. 4:12.

[12] The first paragraph of the book also hints at this narrative when it says, "What is more difficult—to awaken someone who is sleeping or to awaken someone who, awake, is dreaming that he is awake" (*Works of Love*, 5)?

next section, will help unveil the narrative pattern of repetition that structures *Works of Love*.

The Implied Reader's Faith. The preface of *Works of Love* begins by insisting that its deliberations are *Christian* deliberations. It announces that its genuine reader is one who is capable of discerning and judging how well Kierkegaard articulates the essentially Christian.[13] Kierkegaard elsewhere presents Christ and the essentially Christian as a paradox that evokes one of only two honest responses: offense and faith. *Works of Love* presents the essentially Christian in the form of God's paradoxical command to love the neighbor. If the reader discerns the essentially Christian, and yet does not take offense at the paradox, then he must respond in faith. Offense sees the command to love as alienating, as threatening, as a cause for anger or bitterness, and so on. Faith sees it instead as liberating, as a cause for joy and gratitude, as "the only thing worth living for."[14] *Works of Love* moves the reader to deeper faith and love by forcing him to recognize how far removed from the faith he professes are his actions, responses, and perceptions with regard to his neighbor. Because the reader is a primary character in *Works of Love's* narrative, faith also underlies its treatment of many, if not all, of its key themes. A careful reading of the prayer that introduces *Works of Love* suggests that Christian love depends on Christian faith for its fecundity, its commitment to obedience and its recognition of authority, and its self-denying form.

The prayer that follows the preface reveals that the implied reader's faith concerns a God without whom one cannot "speak properly about love." Kierkegaard's writings are

---

[13] Kierkegaard, *Works of Love*, 3.
[14] Ibid., 375.

filled with prayers and thoughts on prayer,[15] but they are seldom as specifically Christian in form as the prayer at the beginning of *Works of Love*.[16] In a clearly Trinitarian idiom, it addresses God as the source of love, Christ as the revealer of love, and the Holy Spirit as the "Spirit of Love," who "remind[s] us of [Christ's] love-sacrifice, remind[s] the believer to love as he is loved and his neighbor as himself." It continues, "O Eternal Love...be not without witness in what will be said here about love or about the works of love." In closing, the prayer recalls again the sacrifice of Christ, by identifying works of love as "sincere in self-renunciation." Finally, it insists that such self-renunciation can never be supererogatory, since it is "a need in love itself, and for that very reason without any claim of meritoriousness."[17] According to this prayer, then, God originates, reveals, and "loves forth" love to and in humans, himself existing as Trinity and so as love. This love has a cruciform shape, desiring to re-enact the complete self-donation of the "Savior and Redeemer," who "gave [himself] in order to save all."

This prayer announces several key themes of the work as whole and places them in the context of the reader's professed

---

[15] For a collection of Kierkegaard's prayers, see Perry D. LeFevre, ed., *The Prayers of Kierkegaard* (Chicago: University of Chicago Press, 1956; rep. 1963).

[16] My analysis of this prayer and its connection to the rest of the text reveals my disagreement with the view that Kierkegaard's use of theological language should be viewed as poetic license and contrasted with the way in which such representatives of Kierkegaard's Christian tradition as St. Paul, St. Augustine, St. Thomas Aquinas, or Martin Luther used the same language. For a view opposing mine, see Wanda Warren Berry, "Finally Forgiveness: Kierkegaard as a 'Springboard' for a Feminist Theology of Reform," in *Foundations of Kierkegaard's Vision of Community: Religion, Ethics, and Politics in Kierkegaard*, ed. George B. Connell and C. Stephen Evans (New Jersey: Humanities Press, 1992), especially 198. For an account elaborating a view similar to mine, see Murray Rae, *Kierkegaard and Theology* (New York: T&T Clark, 2010), especially 166–72.

[17] Kierkegaard, *Works of Love*, 3–4.

faith. First, it suggests that love bears Christian fruit only when planted in the soil of Christian faith. The prayer itself, of course, implies faith on the part of the reader. Kierkegaard notes in a journal entry of 1850 that prayer and faith mutually implicate one another.[18] Other passages in *Works of Love* also signal the presence of faith in the reader. For example, the first paragraph contrasts the dangerous sagacity that insists on walking by sight so as to avoid being deceived with the simple faith that reaches out to love in spite of the danger of deception.[19] That deliberation ends with the claim that one cannot see love unless one first believes in love.[20] If one keeps in mind the prayer that immediately precedes this deliberation, one realizes that this faith in love is also a faith in the God who is the source and revealer of love as well as the one who evokes love from those who live in faith. In a later deliberation, Kierkegaard argues that love from "a sincere faith" requires the self-knowledge one receives only by becoming transparent before God. He asks rhetorically, "If two people are to love each other in sincere faith, is it not simply necessary that honesty before God must first be present in each individual?"[21] If Kierkegaard is to move the implied reader to love, the reader must first be marked by faith.

The prayer at the beginning of *Works of Love* further suggests that faith gladly sees God as worthy of obedience. In doing so, it anticipates the key themes of authority, command, and obedience that pervade the book.[22] Those themes are not

---

[18] Kierkegaard, *Journals*, 3:3456.

[19] Kierkegaard, *Works of Love*, 5.

[20] Ibid., 16.

[21] Ibid., 151.

[22] C. Stephen Evans rightly emphasizes these themes in "Authority and Transcendence in *Works of Love*," in *Kierkegaard Studies Yearbook 1998*, ed. Niels Jorgen Cappelorn and Hermann Deuser with C. Stephen Evans, Alastair Hannay, and Bruce H. Kirmmse (New York: Walter de Gruyter, 1998). Evans

explicitly mentioned in the prayer, but the structure of faith contains them implicitly. As already noted, Kierkegaard believes that prayer both expresses faith and strengthens it. But as an expression of faith, prayer is also a commitment to obedience to divine authority. Kierkegaard writes in his journals, "The true pray-er is simply *obedient*."[23] An upbuilding discourse published a few months before *Works of Love*, makes the point even more clearly. "[F]aith and faith's obedience in sufferings love forth the growth [of one's spirit], because the object of all faith's work is to get rid of egotism and selfishness in order that God can actually come in and in order to let him rule in everything."[24] Faith is oriented toward obedience, so that Kierkegaard can even say, "[I]n obedience faith is faith."[25] Consequently, in *Works of Love*, Kierkegaard does not attempt to justify divine authority or convince his reader that divine authority plays an indispensable role in the moral life. He can set aside those questions because his reader is presumably already a pray-er and so one who sees with the eyes of faith the joys of obedience.[26]

Finally, the introductory prayer anticipates the cruciform shape of the love God commands and its significance as the ultimate horizon for the meaning of human relationships.[27] Christ's sacrifice forms the center of the prayer and anticipates the self-denying character of Christian love. According to the prayer, God "spared nothing but in love gave everything,"

---

elaborates his analysis further in his *Kierkegaard's Ethic of Love: Divine Commands and Moral Obligation* (New York: Oxford University Press, 2006).

[23] Kierkegaard, *Journals*, 3:3403.

[24] Kierkegaard, *Upbuilding Discourses*, 259.

[25] Ibid., 263.

[26] Compare the title of the piece in *Upbuilding Discourses* from which these quotes are taken: "The Joy of It That the School of Suffering Educates for Eternity."

[27] Kierkegaard, *Works of Love*, 375.

even his Son, who in turn "gave [himself] in order to save all." Now the "Spirit of love" "take[s] nothing of [his] own but remind[s] us of that love-sacrifice." The reminder of Christ's sacrifice is at the same time a reminder to "the believer to love as he is loved and his neighbor as himself." To love in that way is to love "sincere[ly] in self-renunciation," which turns out to be "a need in love itself."[28] The prayer presents the external mission of the Trinity as consisting in self-donation, even to the point of sacrifice.[29] The believer is commanded to participate in that task by loving his neighbor in a self-denying kind of way. But that command seems, in some sense, more like an invitation or a permission than an onerous burden, given the high privilege of participation in the divine mission and love's own desire for self-renouncing self-donation. In *Works of Love*'s conclusion, Kierkegaard notes this sense in the "intermediate tone" of the Apostle John's plea, "Beloved, let us love one another."[30] Kierkegaard imagines the apostle explaining this tone by saying, "The commandment is that you *shall* love, but ah, if you will understand yourself and life, then it seems that it should not need to be commanded, because to love people is the only thing worth living for, and without this love you are not really living."[31] God has made humans for just what he commands them to do. Faith sees self-denying love, according to the divine command, as the privilege of participation in the Trinity's own mission and so a cause for joy and gratitude.

---

[28] Ibid., 3–4.

[29] See also ibid., 121: "The love-relationship requires threeness: the lover, the beloved, the love—but the love is God." This sentence echoes Augustine's famous discovery of a trace of the Trinity in the relational structure of love: love goes out from the lover in love to the beloved, just as the Father loves the Son—and the Son, the Father—in the Holy Spirit. See *De Trinitate* Book VII, ch. 10, sect. 14 and XV, 6, 10.

[30] Kierkegaard, *Works of Love*, 375.

[31] Ibid.

The implied reader, whose prayer opens the door to *Works of Love*, already has a beginning in the virtue of faith. One might think that precisely that kind of reader has no need for the pedagogy of *Works of Love*. If one has faith, and so a commitment to obedience and a perception of God's command as a source of joy, then what more has one to learn? But Kierkegaard notes that even Christ "learned obedience."[32] Not surprisingly then, Kierkegaard's aim is to "help others (in such a way as one person can help another, since God is the true helper) to become Christians in an even deeper sense." Doing so means making others "conscious" of the weekday commitments entailed by the Sunday faith they profess.[33] The reader's faith, then, is not complete but still in the process of formation. The reader is not yet aware of its full meaning and significance. *Works of Love* aims to awaken the reader from the moral slumber that obscures faith's deepest meanings and keeps his weekdays distinct from his Sundays.[34] By making the reader aware of the truths the prayer enunciates, and their significance, it hopes to help him "become Christian in a deeper sense," as he learns obedience to the law of love. But this aim suggests that the implied reader is not already characterized by love in any complete way. Instead, as the text bears out, the implied reader comes to the text in the grip of a vice, the vice of improper self-love.

The Implied Reader's Improper Self-Love. The reader has not yet been so transformed by his faith that he loves Christianly, but he does nevertheless love. Kierkegaard identifies as the

---

[32] Hebrews 5:8, the text for "The School of Suffering."

[33] Kierkegaard, *Works of Love*, 48. Kierkegaard associates this task of awakening with the genre of deliberation, in which *Works of Love* is written, as opposed to that of discourse. See Kierkegaard, *Journals*, 1:641, and Kierkegaard, *Practice in Christianity*, 272, for this genre distinction.

[34] See, for example, Kierkegaard, *Journals*, 1:21.

presupposition of Christian deliberations on love that "every person loves himself."[35] That presupposition does not primarily assert a general claim about the class of human beings. Instead, it uncovers the reader's own moral and spiritual state. To read this properly, the reader must think, not "All human beings love themselves," but "I love myself—and perhaps do so badly." Consequently, the succeeding deliberations do not aim primarily to draw conclusions from the presupposition, but to provide a mirror in which the reader can see, and condemn, himself.

Because the implied reader is already someone professing Christian faith but who also needs to "become Christian in a deeper sense," Kierkegaard depicts the particular shape improper self-love has when it manifests itself in a Christian life. In that context, self-love is fundamentally a kind of moral blindness or self-deception. Just as prayer and faith form a kind of virtuous circle, so blind self-love and the fragmentation of the self form a vicious circle. Fragmentation expresses itself in the arbitrary and unstable but unquestioned preferences characteristic of self-love, and they in turn further divide the self. Kierkegaard's condemnation of self-love in the reader depends on that self-destructive circle, rather than on, for example, its failure to embrace the greatest possible number of persons or its self-regard.

The first deliberation of *Works of Love* introduces the essential themes of the book, and its first paragraphs contain some of its most significant images and metaphors. The first sentence makes reference to the disconcerting possibility of deception and the power of "our physical eyes."[36] Later in the paragraph, Kierkegaard moves back and forth between

---

[35] Kierkegaard, *Works of Love*, 17.
[36] Ibid., 5.

metaphors of vision and metaphors of sleep, dreaming, and wakefulness. The rest of the book repeats these themes and images, modulating their contexts and meanings, and relating them to love. Kierkegaard first employs them to describe different kinds of deception. With their help, Kierkegaard enlists the reader in a condemnation of self-deception, so that the reader can later condemn himself when he recognizes his own duplicity.

To begin, Kierkegaard distinguishes two kinds of deception. The first is the straightforward case of "believing what is untrue," for example, that one's beloved loves one when in fact the beloved loves another. To avoid such illusions, one who fears love's epistemic vulnerability may restrict belief to that which one's "physical eyes" can see. Adopting this tactic, one would never fall into the trap of mistaking one's beloved's affections. Since they cannot be seen with the physical eyes, one simply never believes they exist to begin with. As a defense against deception, argues Kierkegaard, this tactic fails, "since we certainly are also deceived by not believing what is true."[37] As a strategy for avoiding unhappy love, such a drastic narrowing of epistemic vision also defeats itself because it prevents recognition of genuinely requited love. Consequently, the attempt to avoid deception traps one in deception even more inextricably.

This trap is the second kind of deception, and it is worse than the first, since it is a kind of self-deception. Since one's own tactics for avoiding deception lead one into deception, one is unlikely to realize one's epistemic predicament. Kierkegaard employs sleep metaphors to suggest how deeply entrenched in self-deception one can become: "What is more difficult—to awaken someone who is sleeping or to awaken someone who,

[37] Ibid.

awake, is dreaming that he is awake?"[38] With this convoluted metaphor, Kierkegaard both describes the tangled mess of self-deception and announces his own task. Paraphrased, he asks, "What is more difficult—to make someone aware of the truth about love who previously had no understanding of it? Or to make someone aware of the truth who has a partial understanding yet falsely believes himself to be fully alive to the whole truth about love?" The second alternative, the more difficult one, constitutes Kierkegaard's task. He must make the implied reader aware of the truth about Christian love even though the reader, as a professing Christian, already believes himself to know it.

Kierkegaard, as I have noted, begins by showing the inadequacies of a view that limits belief only to those things that the physical eyes can see. These opening comments may seem at first glance less than helpful, since no one, or almost no one, advocates this degree of epistemic discipline. Even the logical positivists did not insist that one believe only what one can see with one's physical eyes, a view that would have committed them to the denial of the existence of subatomic particles as well as of moral realities like love. Besides, after the preface and introductory prayer, Kierkegaard is likely already to have lost any reader inclined to such extremes of suspicion. Taken as a piece of straightforward philosophical argument, this opening gambit is at best tilting at straw men.

But it has a purpose in the context of Kierkegaard's pedagogical goals and the character of the implied reader. In that context, the opening paragraphs achieve two effects. First, they enlist the reader in an easy condemnation of self-deception, preparatory to revealing, in later deliberations, the reader's own self-deception in self-love. Already in the second

[38] Ibid.

paragraph, Kierkegaard begins gently to unsettle the reader who has just gotten comfortable in seeing through those others who mistakenly think they see through love. The self-deception Kierkegaard uncovers in the reader is even more tangled than the first two kinds the reader has already condemned. The reader, despite his profession of Christian faith, actually sees other loves as higher than the love God commands and displays in his Trinitarian mission. In the second deliberation, Kierkegaard challenges the reader,

> Make the test here: forget Christianity for a moment and think of what you ordinarily know as love; call to mind what you read in the poets, what you yourself can find out, and then say whether it ever occurred to you to think this: You *shall* love? ...Be honest, admit that most people, when they read the poets' glowing description of erotic love or friendship, it is perhaps the case that this seems to be something far higher than this poor: "You *shall* love."[39]

The Christian faith articulated in the introductory prayer finds the love of God as revealed in Christ's sacrifice as the most significant love, the context that makes speaking "properly" of love at all possible.[40] But Kierkegaard's Christian reader, though assenting to that prayer with apparent sincerity, actually sees love differently, really finding the beauty of erotic love or friendship more compelling than the rigors of Christian love.

Kierkegaard, then, has described three kinds of deception, each progressively more complex and each implicating more deeply the character of the deceived. The first kind of deception occurs when one person deceives another about the genuineness of the first person's love for the second. One

---

[39] Ibid., 29.
[40] Ibid., 3.

strategy for avoiding that kind of deception results in the second kind of deception that occurs when a person, eager to avoid being deceived in the first way, refuses to believe love exists even when it does. To avoid such self-deception, Kierkegaard insists that one must have a heart formed by love, because only love can see love. The third kind of deception occurs when a person convinces himself his heart is formed by one kind of love when an entirely different sort actually shapes it. This is the most pernicious form of self-deception because most people lack the perception to distinguish accurately between the different kinds of love or to see clearly their relative significance.[41] Kierkegaard aims to equip his reader with those abilities; hence, he challenges the reader to "be honest" about the reader's perception of the different loves and their significance. Having already secured his reader's condemnation of self-deception, this challenge has bite to it.

Failing to meet that challenge, the reader inevitably deceives himself about the state of his own soul. Speaking of the "poet," Kierkegaard says, "he cannot understand himself or understand that he himself is a riddle." Kierkegaard predicts that such a person, if "compelled" to confront the truth about himself and his loves, would "become indignant and embittered" or sadly reject the knowledge as useless.[42] This image summarizes one possibility for the reader's story.[43]

---

[41] Kierkegaard would not underestimate "Christendom's" role in rendering people impotent in this regard. That observation links *Works of Love* to the later "attack on Christendom."

[42] Kierkegaard, *Works of Love*, 30.

[43] In the anger and bitterness of those who refuse to acknowledge the truth, and in the compulsion necessary to turn someone toward the truth, this image is reminiscent of the philosopher's journey in the cave allegory of Plato's *Republic* (Book VII). The cave allegory, in turn, recalls Socrates's tragic end at the hands of the Athenians and anticipates Kierkegaard's own struggles in his "attack on Christendom."

Having been confronted with the truth about his existence, the reader may respond with anger and bitterness or simply reject the knowledge, and attempt to continue living in a now more directly willed duplicity. But, though the reader unconsciously lives the "poet's" existence through the confusion of his loves, he need not come to the poet's end. His faith may still make it possible for him to reject duplicity and live a more genuinely Christian existence. Thus, the theme of self-deception announced in the opening paragraph underwrites the narrative structure of the work as a whole and pinpoints the transition it requires the reader to make.[44]

The reader's self-deception also makes him unable to see his relation to others clearly. The honest reader, after admitting that he does really find erotic love and friendship more compelling, more significant, than Christian love, can now see himself in the comments about erotic love that Kierkegaard makes earlier in the second deliberation. The poets celebrate those who love their beloveds *more than themselves*. But God commands that one love one's neighbor *as oneself*.[45] Though Christian love seems at first somewhat paltry compared to the poetic, Kierkegaard insists that the appearance does not reflect the reality, since poetic love does not actually love the beloved even *as oneself*, much less *more than oneself*. Poetic love, after all, would not be willing to give up the relationship to the beloved for the good of the beloved, since doing so would suggest poetic love is not of ultimate significance.[46] "The [poetic] lover

[44] On this level, Kierkegaard recalls Socrates. Many of Socrates's dialogues may be read as attempts to make the self-deceptions and self-contradictions of his interlocutors clear, so that they must decide whether to continue willfully in a fragmented life or to adjust their beliefs and commitments in pursuit of the true and the good. *Works of Love* serves a similar function.

[45] Kierkegaard, *Works of Love*, 18–19.

[46] Ibid., 21.

thinks that he loves the other person even more than himself,"[47] but he deceives himself.

Finally, the reader's self-deception prevents him from recognizing the true value of others. Christian love requires one to see and to love others as "neighbors," but self-love cannot assimilate the concept of a neighbor.[48] Self-love cannot see another *as* the neighbor but only as friend or beloved or so on. The reader, then, tangled up in his confusion about the nature of his loves, with his heart formed by the wrong kind of love, cannot see others as they really are, that is, as neighbors.

Kierkegaard's analysis of these kinds of deception depends on visual metaphors that proliferate throughout the book. He begins with a reference to physical eyes and physical vision but in such a way that the reader is at once disabused of the notion that physical sight is relevant in matters of love and turned to a more inward kind of sight. Having procured the reader's agreement in rejecting a self-defeating strategy for avoiding deception, Kierkegaard describes love as hidden from sight, but recognizable by its fruits.[49] A replacement technique seems to be in the offing, one that would rely on the presence or absence of fruits to avoid deception about love, but Kierkegaard disappoints that hope. Instead, Kierkegaard argues that no particular word or work "can unconditionally be said to demonstrate unconditionally the presence of love or to demonstrate unconditionally its absence."[50] Since love is hidden and recognizable only in its ambiguous fruits, external techniques will be no help in discerning its presence.

[47] Ibid.

[48] Ibid. See also p. 89.

[49] Kierkegaard, *Works of Love*, 8–9.

[50] Ibid., 14. But see also p. 7: "[Y]ou will recognize love by its fruits: by the bitterness of the mockery, by the acridity of the sensibleness, by the poisonous sprit of distrust, by the biting cold of callousness—that is, it will be recognizable from the fruits that there is no love within."

Consequently, Kierkegaard turns his attention to the heart. "Love *forms* the heart,"[51] and only a heart formed by love can see love in another.[52] So, Kierkegaard turns the reader away from a search for external techniques as defenses against deception to an inward examination of the reader's own heart. One might say that he has turned attention from physical eyes to the eyes of the heart.

Combining the diagnosis of self-deception with the metaphors of vision suggests that the reader suffers from a perceptual defect or even moral blindness. And, in fact, this characterization of the reader lies in the background of the early deliberations. Consider, for example, Kierkegaard's description of erotic love as "the beautiful dizziness of infinity"[53] as he unmasks the selfishness behind the poetic claim that erotic lovers love the beloved or the friend even more than themselves. Dizziness is at root a visual metaphor, as these remarks from papers roughly contemporary with *Works of Love* show:

> Dizziness, as has been pointed out with physiological correctness, occurs when the eyes have no fixed point upon which to rest. Therefore one becomes dizzy by looking down from a high tower, because the gaze plunges down and finds no boundary, no limitation. Thus when a person notices that he is becoming dizzy, he can stop it by fixing his eyes upon something particular. ...In the spiritual sense,...[dizziness] can be occasioned by a person's going so far astray in the infinite

[51] Kierkegaard, *Works of Love*, 12.
[52] Ibid., 16.
[53] Ibid., 19.

that nothing finite can have continuance for him, that he can find no criterion.[54]

Erotic love is dizzy in this sense. By aiming to love the beloved "more than oneself" or even "more than God," the erotic lover establishes no boundaries for his love. A limitless love of another human being has no context within which to matter and no goal towards which to move beyond the satisfaction of some hidden drive or desire of the self.[55] Hence, says Kierkegaard, "the love [the poets] celebrate is secretly self-love."[56] Commanded love remedies the dizziness of celebrated love by defining the neighbor as the "other" whom one ought to love as one loves oneself. The neighbor thus provides a "fixed point" on which the eyes of the heart can focus. Insofar as the reader is self-deceptively tangled in erotic love, his problem is perceptual, a lack of visual focus, spiritually understood. The perceptual defects, even blindness, of self-love will become clearer to the reader when Kierkegaard describes more fully the lucid vision of Christian love, relying even more heavily on visual metaphors.

Kierkegaard imagines the reader caught in a web of self-deception. The reader deceives himself about the type of love that forms his heart and, in turn, his misshapen heart prevents him from seeing the truth about his relations to others and

---

[54] Quoted in Søren Kierkegaard, *The Book on Adler*, trans. and ed. Howard V. Hong and Edna H. Hong (Princeton NJ: Princeton University Press, 1998) 287–88.

[55] See Anti-Climacus's discussion of the criterion of the self in Søren Kierkegaard, *Sickness Unto Death: A Christian Psychological Exposition for Upbuilding and Awakening*, trans. and ed. Howard V. Hong and Edna H. Hong (Princeton NJ: Princeton University Press, 1983) 79–83.

[56] Kierkegaard, *Works of Love*, 19. See also p. 55, where Kierkegaard specifically identifies the limitlessness (that is, the dizziness in the sense just specified) of poetic love as the factor that makes it a form of self-love: "[I]n his impetuous, unlimited devotion, the lover is actually relating himself to himself in self-love."

about others' true significance. *Works of Love* also implies that such self-deception proceeds from and fosters a basic fragmentation of the self. A key text for this claim is the following:

> In erotic love the *I* is defined as sensate-psychical-spiritual; the beloved is a sensate-psychical-spiritual specification. In friendship the *I* is defined as psychical-spiritual; the friend is a psychical-spiritual specification. It is only in love for the neighbor that the self, who loves, is defined as spirit purely spiritually and the neighbor is a purely spiritual specification. ...In the beloved and the friend, it of course is not the neighbor who is loved, but the *other I*, or the first *I* once again, but more intensely.[57]

Kierkegaard contrasts the self-deceptive loves of the reader with neighbor love, in which both subject and object are "purely spiritual." Kierkegaard does not mean simply to oppose neighbor love to the body or to the flesh, understood as matter. To the contrary, he writes, "By the sensuous, the flesh, Christianity understands selfishness. A conflict between spirit and flesh is inconceivable unless there is a rebellious spirit on the side of flesh, with which the spirit then contends."[58] Neighbor love is spiritual not because it neglects or represses the physical, but because it overcomes a conflict deep in the self.

Spirit, then, is opposed to inner conflict and suggests some sort of unity. Other texts reveal that "spirit" names the human capacity for becoming self-integrated around the self's relation to the eternal.[59] In *The Sickness Unto Death*, Kierkegaard

---

[57] Kierkegaard, *Works of Love*, 56–57.

[58] Ibid., 52. See also Kierkegaard, *Journals*, 4:4354.

[59] See also Kierkegaard, *Journals*, 4:4340 and 4:4352, and Kierkegaard, *Sickness Unto Death*, 107: "Every existence that is within the qualification spirit, even if only on its own responsibility and at its own risk, has an essential

explains that a human being is a synthesis of the sensate, or physical, and the psychical, and that each human can become conscious of himself as a synthesis. When this synthesis relates itself to itself before another, it achieves a kind of unity that provides a context of meaning for the two elements of the synthesis. In so doing, one becomes spirit. The human being is a synthesis capable of becoming spirit, but not the cause of its own existence or the source of its own meaning. Spirit's relation to "the power that established it" completes it by situating it within a larger horizon, so that its relation to the synthesis that makes it up is not merely arbitrary.[60] Kierkegaard identifies the establishing power as God and a positive relation to God as faith.[61]

When Kierkegaard describes the various loves as sensate-psychical-spiritual, psychical-spiritual, or as purely spiritual, he is describing them in terms of their relation to the unity of the self. Every human being is a spirit of sorts.[62] So every human love is, in that sense, spiritual. But every human also has as a task becoming a spirit in a more definite sense. The loves Kierkegaard describes differ in the degree of unity they presuppose and foster in the self; that is, they differ in their contribution to the essentially human task of becoming spirit. Erotic love fails to integrate the sensate and psychical dimensions of the self, since the significance of its response to the sensuous appeal of the beloved remains independent of, and even determines, its psyche. Friendship fails to integrate the psychical dimension of the self, since its affections by

interior consistency and a consistency in something higher, at least in an idea." Others, however, "never experience putting everything together on one thing, never achieve the idea of an infinite self-consistency."

[60] Kierkegaard, *Sickness Unto Death*, 13–14.

[61] Ibid., 82.

[62] Ibid., 13; see also Kierkegaard, *Postscript*, 1:131.

themselves determine the whole self's commitments.[63] Only neighbor love makes possible a unified, purely spiritual self, since it integrates the sensate and psychical into the spirit's faith, so that neither dimension of the self arbitrarily determines the significance of the lover and the neighbor independently of its place in the unified self as a whole. The genuinely Christian lover, spirit in a more definite sense, acts as a unified self and views others also as spirits in relation to God.[64]

One may recast these claims in the vocabulary the last chapter introduced in the account of the emotions. To be spirit is to be a person of fully developed character. The two dimensions of the self, the sensate and the psychical, differentiate two families of concerns.[65] Sensate concerns are concerns for sensuous satisfactions; psychical concerns are concerns for experiences of affection, bonds of common purpose and activity, and so on. To love someone sensately-psychically-spiritually is to see them and relate to them in terms of one's sensate concerns. To love someone psychically-spiritually is to see them and relate to them in terms of one's psychical concerns. To become spirit, a fully developed character, is to find some fundamental concern that can make sense of all the others and integrate them into a whole. Neither sensate nor psychical concerns can make sense, in their own

---

[63] Both of these loves are, consequently, forms of despair. See Kierkegaard, *Works of Love*, 40: "The despair is due to relating oneself with infinite passion to a particular something, for one can relate oneself with infinite passion—unless one is in despair—only to the eternal."

[64] See Kierkegaard, *Works of Love*, 219, and the whole deliberation, "Love Builds Up."

[65] *Sickness Unto Death* would require speaking not only of families of concerns but also of families of abilities and conditions—for example, the condition of being historically situated and the ability to transcend that historical situation in imagination.

terms, of their opposite numbers, and neither enables the self to view itself whole. Kierkegaard believes that only one concern, a concern for one's God-relation, has the possibility of integrating the self and its concerns (and even then, only when it is developed positively as faith rather than negatively as offense).

But why not think that one can simply add these sensate and psychical concerns together so as to arrive at a complex but complete self? Why think that these various concerns must all be unified around one fundamental concern? One may imagine a reader at this point simply rejecting the ideal of self-unity Kierkegaard advocates, preferring a picture of the self as an aggregate, including as much diversity as possible within moral limits, rather than as an integrated whole. Consider the following remarks from John Rawls's *A Theory of Justice*: "[A] rational plan [of life] will include many (or at least several) final aims."[66] One constructs a rational plan of life by including as many ends as possible, though one cannot order the most inclusive set of ends towards any one dominant end. Rawls reasons, "Human good is heterogeneous because the aims of the self are heterogeneous. Although to subordinate all our aims to one end does not strictly speaking violate the principles of rational choice…, it still strikes us as irrational, or more likely as mad. The self is disfigured and put in the service of one of its ends for the sake of system."[67] Rawls calls this objectionable view of the human good the "dominant end" theory, giving Ignatius Loyola and Thomas Aquinas as examples of its advocates.[68] He argues that its attraction comes from its promise of "a method of choice which the agent

[66] John Rawls, *A Theory of Justice* (Cambridge MA: The Belknap Press of Harvard University Press, 1971) 549.

[67] Rawls, *A Theory of Justice*, 554.

[68] Ibid., 552–54.

himself can always follow in order to make a rational decision," so that "only difficulties of computation and lack of information remain."[69] Rawls argues that all such attempts fail because the candidates for dominant end are either so inhuman as to be wildly implausible or so vague as to be of no help in eliminating the disputes standing in the way of a rational, quantitative decision-making procedure.[70] One instead must find the unity of the self not in any end or system of ends but in "the principles that we would acknowledge to govern the background conditions under which these aims are to be formed and the manner in which they are to be pursued."[71]

Since he would surely consider Kierkegaard's view a version of a dominant end theory, Rawls's comments can provide a foil for the distinctive aspects of Kierkegaard's approach.[72] First, Rawls misses the point of "dominant end theories" such as Kierkegaard's. Kierkegaard is not searching for a method of choice that relies only on quantitative "counting principles." Instead, Kierkegaard is attempting to articulate a form of human existence embodying Christian claims about God and human nature. Rather than pursuing quantitative methods of decision-making, Kierkegaard insists again and again that becoming a self in the fullest sense requires qualitative transformations. Second, Rawls complains that theologically oriented dominant end theories leave the dominant end vague, but Kierkegaard's entire authorship can be read as a specification of what it means to have an "infinite passion" for one's relation to God. Of course, Kierkegaard's

[69] Ibid., 552.

[70] Ibid., 553–54.

[71] Ibid., 560.

[72] Compare, for instance, his report of Loyola's criticism of attachments to objects other than God with Kierkegaard's own hard sayings about self-denial and detachment cited above in the discussion of the implied reader's improper self-love.

authorship does not direct particular choices; but there's no reason to think it should, once one realizes it does not intend to present a quantitative method of choice. Nor does his work eliminate the need for continuing argument about authentic human existence, but neither does it claim to.

So Kierkegaard's project, along with others relevantly similar to it, does not provide a suitable target for Rawls's criticisms of dominant-end quantitative rationality. But neither is Kierkegaard's work an example of Rawls's alternative model of inclusive life-plans. Kierkegaard's thoughts suggest another approach, one that does not focus on aims, ends, and rational decision-making, as Rawls uses those terms, but instead on the perceptions of meaning and significance within which one acts. One's perceptions of significance, typically experienced as emotions, depend on one's concerns, or passions, as Kierkegaard often calls them. To be concerned for one's God-relation is not quite the same thing as having it as an end to which everything else is subordinated as an instrumental means. Since Kierkegaard emphasizes becoming a person with the proper passions more than achieving certain ends, the kind of subordination he recommends in the moral life is not the means-end relation Rawls envisages. To take one of Rawls's own examples, on Kierkegaard's view, play and recreation are not merely means towards the end of faith, but activities that receive their significance in light of one's concern for one's God-relation. In that light, one comes to enjoy recreation not as a merely permissible means to another end but as a source of joy or pleasure in light of one's constitution as a synthesis of finite and infinite in relation to God. One takes one's amusements lightly, with humor, since their contrast with one's relation to God relativizes them. Nonetheless, one fully engages them, as might an adult take seriously but lightly a game played with children. Finding the right stance towards recreation does not necessarily entail finding its suitability as a means to some dominant end, but instead correctly apprehending its significance in the light of one's concern for the most important thing.[73]

This orientation toward passion rather than means-end calculation explains why Kierkegaard rejects any model that builds one's inclusive end through addition. Kierkegaard writes, "Erotic love and friendship are related to passion but all passion, whether it attacks or defends itself, fights in one way only, either/or: 'Either I exist and am the highest or I do not exist at all, either all or nothing.'"[74] According to Kierkegaard, the passions, or at least the passions most relevant to a person's loves, have a tendency to become so fundamental that they set the context for more and more of one's questions of meaning. In this case, one cannot simply add together erotic love, friendship, and neighbor love to achieve one inclusive love. Instead, erotic love has its own dynamic tendency to become the concern in terms of which one sees oneself and others. So, too, do friendship and neighbor love. The question, then, is which is to be "dethroned" or "enthroned." Kierkegaard's concern is not with arranging ends and means into a hierarchy that provides a quantitative rational choice procedure. Instead he focuses on the challenge presented by the expanding passions of the self. Some form of love will shape the passions of the heart, the deep structure of one's concerns and attachments, so that one sees oneself and others in terms of certain basic concerns. One cannot simply add them together because they are dynamic, tending to prompt one's construals for more and more of one's world. They are essentially in

[73] Kierkegaard, *Postscript*, 1:413, 495–97.

[74] Kierkegaard, *Works of Love*, 45.

conflict, each with imperialistic ambitions and none providing more reason than any other for their ascendancy.

The necessary conflict internal to a heart that refuses to decide between ultimate passions also explains Kierkegaard's insistence that self-love is the product of "drives" and "inclinations." For example, he contrasts self-love with Christian love in the following way: "What a difference there is between the play of feelings, drives, inclinations, and passions, in short, that play of the powers of immediacy, that celebrated glory of poetry in smiles or in tears, in desire or in want—what a difference between this and the earnestness of the commandment in spirit and truth, in honesty and self-denial!"[75] In another place, he writes, "Erotic love is based on a drive (*Drift*) transfigured into an inclination (*Tilboielighed*)."[76] In these passages, Kierkegaard refers to a family of concerns that the reader experiences as given, as a kind of instinct, though one can become more or less conscious of their determining influence. In this context, when one becomes aware of a drive or instinct as given, it has become an inclination. Though Kierkegaard gives the reader no reason to reject inclination as such, it can become problematic for those learning to love Christianly. When one does not recognize the defeasibility of an inclination, it tends to assert itself as unquestionable and as the ultimate context for all other concerns and perceptions.

Compare, for example, the inclination to eat and drink with the inclinations to love erotically or in friendship. As Kierkegaard explains, Christianity "has been no more scandalized by a drive human beings have not given to themselves than it has wanted to forbid people to eat and

[75] Ibid., 25.
[76] Ibid., 49.

drink."[77] A concern for self-preservation provides the basis for a construal of food and drink as of great significance, but one experiences that perception as instinctual, not requiring choice or even, in ordinary circumstances, justification. If one were to attempt a justification of it that would demonstrate its reliable grasp of the genuine import of food and drink, one would have to place it in a context larger than itself and consider it in relation to other, possibly even more important, concerns, such as religious devotion, loyalty to family, or aspiration to athletic excellence. Those concerns may sometimes reveal the relative insignificance of food and drink.

The poet views erotic love as an instinct like that of eating and drinking, but without providing any larger context from within which to evaluate it. As the poets present it, erotic love is an instinct that properly dominates those who have a beloved and those who lack one but dream of finding one. When erotic love gains an unquestioned ascendancy in one's heart, it reveals each new person as a possibility, assistant, or rival in the search for or enjoyment of romance. For those animated by this concern, the poet brings to expression their perception of an undeniable instinct, transforming it into inclination. The instinctive concern for friendship similarly facilitates a construal of others according to which one finds their suitability or lack thereof for companionship with oneself to be their most significant quality. Erotic love and friendship, then, lead their possessor to construe the significance of others in terms of their own basic concerns for sensuous satisfaction, whether more or less sophisticated, or for companionship. To justify either inclination would require the reader to resolve their conflict over the right to the highest place in his heart, a conflict neither love can win with finality apart from a point of

[77] Ibid., 52.

view that can encompass both. The implied reader's erotic love and friendships appear to him as givens because of his self-fragmentation into rival and unintegrated instinctual drives.

Kierkegaard often refers to the reader's erotic and friendship loves as "preferential" and means that as a derogatory remark. If one keeps in mind the picture of the reader's self as divided among various drives and inclinations, each of which aims to set the terms for the whole self, one can see why the preferential nature of the reader's loves constitutes a defect. Otherwise, one may think that Kierkegaard finally endorses only that love that diffuses itself equally to every person. A passage from Jonathan Edwards suggests the sentiment this mistaken interpretation attributes to Kierkegaard: "[T]he nature of true virtue consists in a disposition to benevolence towards being in general; though from such a disposition may arise exercises of love to particular beings, as objects are presented and occasions arise."[78] Gilbert Meilaender explains this ordering of loves as a strategy—represented by Edwards, Jeremy Taylor, and, perhaps, Kierkegaard—of "building down" from a basic, non-preferential Christian love to the preferential, particular loves of romance and friendship. He assumes that such thinkers believe non-preferential or "private" loves lack the universality of object of genuinely Christian love, and so must be either derived in some way from Christian love or eliminated altogether. Meilaender opposes this strategy to one of "building up" from particular loves to universal, Christian

[78] Jonathan Edwards, *The Nature of True Virtue* (Ann Arbor: University of Michigan Press, 1960) 5, cited in Gilbert C. Meilaender, *Friendship: A Study in Theological Ethics* (Notre Dame IN: University of Notre Dame Press, 1981) 22–23.

love, proposing Augustine and Joseph Butler as exemplary advocates.[79]

If one construes the "building up" strategy as a matter of adding particular loves together to approximate universal love, then surely Kierkegaard would reject it as falsifying both Christian love and erotic love. On the other hand, Kierkegaard also avoids the "building down" strategy, at least if it is interpreted with the assumption Meilaender makes. Kierkegaard is not much interested in the universality of love's object, in making sure that every person is added in. He insists, to the contrary, that one cannot define Christian love by its object.[80] He is, instead, more interested in the wholeness of the loving self. A whole self will reveal itself in works of Christian love, and a divided, deceived self will manifest in works of lesser loves.[81] The fundamental defect of preferential loves is not first that they have reference only to one or a few rather than to all, but that they issue from a divided self that reveals its division through its exclusions of others. Erotic love and friendship ground construals of their objects in terms of some more or less conscious instinctual drive of the self. For the reader, characterized by such loves, others' significance depends on his own conflicting drives and inclinations, and so he finds others to be of radically differing imports and some of no significance at all. His perceptions of significance are then just as arbitrary as his capitulation to one instinct rather than another. It is for this reason also that Kierkegaard terms erotic love and friendship love species of self-love; they view the

[79] Meilaender, *Friendship*, 16–22, 29–32.

[80] Kierkegaard, *Works of Love*, 66.

[81] Bruce Kirmmse writes, "The Lover, in having to do with others, has essentially to do with him- or herself and learns thereby who he or she is" (*Kierkegaard in Golden Age Denmark* [Bloomington IN: Indiana University Press, 1990] 313). Kirmmse is describing Christian love but his remarks also apply, in a slightly different sense, to the other loves.

significance of others in terms of the self's own divided instincts. In so doing, they, in a sense, incorporate the other into the self, rather than seeing the other's independent significance.[82] A whole self, on the other hand, united by faith's concern for the God-relation, will perceive others' significance in terms of that concern and so find everyone significant in each one's imaging of eternity.[83]

This difference between fragmented and whole selves also explains the instability and characteristic affects of self-love. Consider, for example, jealousy and despair as instances of the instability typical of self-love. The reader possessed by erotic love sees his beloved as significant because she satisfies his instinct for reciprocal sensuous experience. But her ability to satisfy that instinct, the reciprocal nature of their relationship, and even the strength of his own drive can vary and change with time and circumstances, rendering his love dangerously unstable. Furthermore, the jealous reader perceives the significance of his beloved in a kind of anxiety and resentment about their respective engagements in the relationship, tortured by a kind of fear that his involvement exceeds hers. He resents his beloved because he feels himself driven deeper into and becoming more dependent on the relationship than she. Kierkegaard writes of jealous love, "Anxious and tortured by preoccupation with itself, it dares neither to believe the beloved absolutely nor to give itself wholeheartedly, lest it give too much." A love like that, with its obsessive tendencies, may seem more vigorous and passionate, in the colloquial sense, than the humbler but more genuine "simple love." "But," Kierkegaard asks, "is fragmentation stronger than unity; is a heart torn asunder stronger than a whole and undivided heart;

[82] Kierkegaard, *Works of Love*, 55.
[83] Ibid., 89.

does a perpetually anxious grasp hold its object more firmly than the unified powers of simplicity!" Jealousy's apparent vitality is the desperate energy of a chaotic, divided self. Kierkegaard identifies the proximate causes of jealousy as the habit of comparison and the preferential nature of self-love.[84] Preferential love's connection with self-division has already been described. The divided self has no context within which to judge the fittingness of its loving, other than the limitless drive of its own instincts. So it compares itself to others' loving, especially to its own beloved's, in order to find some limits against which to measure and understand itself. Unfortunately, its attempt to escape its own inherent dizziness leads it directly to jealousy, since others' loving is necessarily hidden from its "sidelong glance."[85] Self-love, then, is inherently unstable, always tending to change from happy affection to anxious jealousy.

Kierkegaard also claims that self-love has a tendency to change from innocent happiness to despair, when some misfortune changes its circumstances. When the inclination goes unsatisfied, self-love can only become despair, since it takes for granted the necessity of the inclination that drives it. But Kierkegaard points out that this change is only apparent. "Only that person can despair who is in despair." In other words, self-love's despair at misfortune simply reveals a deeper despair that has characterized it all along. "Despair is a misrelation in a person's innermost being—no fate or event can penetrate so far and so deep; it can only make manifest that the misrelation—was there." Kierkegaard further argues, "The despair is due to relating oneself with infinite passion to a particular something, for one can relate oneself with infinite

[84] Ibid., 35–36.
[85] Ibid., 186.

passion—unless one is in despair—only to the eternal."[86] Those concerns central to self-love are concerns for something finite, something of limited importance, such as romantic liaisons or abiding companionship. When one convinces oneself that they are of unlimited importance, one opens fissures in the self that lead to all the failures of self-love.

So far, reading *Works of Love* from the perspective of "that single individual," the reader, I have surveyed the first three deliberations. Construing the implied reader as a character in a narrative, I have indicated the character qualities with which the reader begins. Characterized from the beginning by a Christian faith, the exposition of the narrative finds the reader tangled in self-deception on several levels. Kierkegaard's depiction of the true nature of the reader's love is also an unmasking of its incompatibility with his faith and of its failure to constitute genuine love. In the fourth deliberation, Kierkegaard draws a clearer picture of the Christian love to which God calls the reader, contrasting its vision of the neighbor with self-love's blindness. Having become aware of the various levels of his self-deception, the reader now begins to understand more fully what Christian love really is. In the next section, I sketch out the picture of Christian love as Kierkegaard's reader begins to grasp it.

The Implied Reader's Emerging Christian Love. Christian love is a complex concept. To love Christianly is to have a certain relationship with one's neighbor but also to possess a stable quality of character.[87] In the fourth deliberation, Kierkegaard emphasizes love as a kind of vision or perception of the true significance of others. Putting these concepts and images

[86] Ibid., 40.

[87] Kierkegaard assumes love is a virtue (*Journals*, 3:2410), classes it with faith (*Journals*, 3:2419, cited in *Works of Love*, 479–80), and refers to it as a disposition (*Works of Love*, 78, 191).

together, one might say that the reader will love Christianly when he has a settled disposition to see everyone he meets as his neighbor, that is, as fundamentally equal to him because both he and his neighbor have the task of becoming spirit before God. Before the reader's relation to this neighbor is a matter of loving action, it is a matter of loving attention. The reader's perception of the neighbor will depend on his own willingness to make his relation with God his fundamental concern or horizon of significance; in other words, seeing others with Christian love requires first relating to God in faith.[88]

This characterization of Christian love depends on three sets of texts. The first set, drawn mostly from Kierkegaard's journals and papers, likens love to faith in that both are stable qualities of the self. Kierkegaard writes, "Just as *faith* is a dialectical specification, so also is true Christian love. Therefore, Christianity teaches very specifically that one ought to love one's enemy."[89] Christianity calls one to believe the unbelievable and to love the unlovable. Becoming a Christian in a deeper sense requires one to take up these dialectical tasks in more genuine and complete ways. But, once taken up, they cannot be finished and superseded. Instead, by taking up the tasks of faith and of love, one makes them a part of one's character. About faith, Kierkegaard writes, "Faith, the man of faith's conflict with the world, is a battle of character. ...The man of faith is a person of character who, unconditionally obedient to God, grasps it as a character-task that one is not to insist upon comprehending."[90] Believing the incomprehensible is not the accomplishment of a moment. As a character-task,

---

[88] "Ultimately, love for God is the decisive factor; from this originates love for the neighbor" (Kierkegaard, *Works of Love*, 57).

[89] Kierkegaard, *Journals*, 3:2419 (cited in Kierkegaard, *Works of Love*, 479).

[90] Kierkegaard, *Journals*, 2:1129.

the battle for faith defines the shape of a person's life over time. Similarly, Christian love is not primarily an abstracted moment of obedience, but a character-task that disposes one to such obedience over time.[91]

Like faith, love is a quality of character, but one of a peculiar sort. Unlike, say, Aristotelian temperance, faith is not simply the perfection of an individual's capacity. Instead, it is a relationship between "God as personality and the believer as *existing* personality."[92] Robert C. Roberts, referring mostly to *Philosophical Fragments* and *Concluding Unscientific Postscript*, explains,

> While faith is a personal trait, and thus analogous to generosity, courage, or truthfulness, it is also a relationship with a particular other person, and thus is a special kind of virtue, in some respects more like friendship, as Aristotle understands it, than like the other virtues. ...In a virtue like friendship, the concerns and patterns of emotional response will take as their primary object the particular other person in the relationship—the friend.[93]

Like faith, love is both a personal trait and a relationship with another person. As virtues, faith and love consist in the concerns and patterns of response that properly take as their object that other person. The person who is the object of faith is specified by the revelation of the God-Man. The person who is the object of erotic love or friendship is specified by the drives and inclinations at the root of those loves, together with the accidents of circumstance. But the person who is the object of

---

[91] Cf. Kierkegaard, *Postscript*, 1:163–64.

[92] Kierkegaard, *Journals*, 1:180.

[93] Robert C. Roberts, "Dialectical Emotions and the Virtue of Faith," in *International Kierkegaard Commentary: Concluding Unscientific Postscript to "Philosophical Fragments,"* ed. Robert L. Perkins (Macon GA: Mercer University Press, 1997) 73.

Christian love is specified by Christ's command. Christian love is a relationship with the neighbor, and the neighbor is whomever I see, that is, the one to whom I have a duty. It is not, by contrast, a love for "humanity" in general. So Christian love has to do with one other person at a time, while rejecting every hint of exclusivity.

Like faith, then, Christian love is a relationship to another person, though not always the same individual. But Christian love is not a relation of two. "Worldly wisdom is of the opinion that love is a relationship between persons; Christianity teaches that love is a relationship between: a person—God—a person, that is, that God is the middle term."[94] One's concern for the neighbor arises and takes its significance from one's relationship to God in faith. Without the God-relation as an ultimate horizon of significance, one's love for one's neighbor would be as arbitrary as any other merely human love. In a two-person relationship, says Kierkegaard, the one who judges the presence and quality of love is the object of love on whose behalf "devotion" and "sacrifice" are shown. "Thus it depends on whether the people who are to judge know how to judge correctly. If, namely, the object of love, the judge, does not by himself before God have a true idea of what it is to love oneself—that it is to love God—then neither does the beloved have a true idea of what it is to be loved by another person, that it is to be helped to love God."[95]

Without God as the middle term, love will lose its meaning as a help toward the unification of the person before God, and become instead a means to the satisfaction of drives or inclinations on the part of the lover or the beloved. Christian

---

[94] Kierkegaard, *Works of Love*, 107. Cf. Kierkegaard, *Journals*, 3:2380, one of the earliest journal entries: "All true love is grounded in this, that one loves another in a third.... [T]he brothers should love one another in Christ."

[95] Kierkegaard, *Works of Love*, 107.

love is a relationship, but it is a relationship among three, so that God can preserve the meaning and significance of love for the human neighbors. Faith and Christian love can be relationships and at the same time stable qualities of character because God's unchangeableness secures the relationships that constitute them.

A second set of passages expands my earlier description of Christian love. These passages demonstrate 1) that love consists in a range of perceptions of the neighbor, 2) based on attachments to God and, under God, to the neighbor, and 3) that those perceptions are typically had in and through the emotions. One key passage, worth quoting at length, is the following:

> [W]hen someone goes with God, he does indeed go without danger; but he is also compelled to see and to see in a unique way. When you go with God, you need to see only one single miserable person and you will be unable to escape what Christianity wants you to understand—human similarity. ...Yes, going with God (and it is indeed only in this company that one discovers *the neighbor,* because God is the middle term) in order to learn to know life and oneself is an earnest walk. Then honor, power, and glory lose their worldly glamour; in company with God you are unable to delight in them in a worldly way. ...But when you go with God, hold only to him, and understand under God everything you understand, then you will discover the neighbor; then God will constrain you to love him—shall I say, to your own detriment—because to love the neighbor is a thankless task.[96]

According to this passage, an attachment to God ("going with God") changes one's perceptions of oneself and others. To go with God is to understand the meaning and significance of

---

[96] Ibid., 77–78.

everything one perceives in relation to one's relation with God. When one understands oneself and one's world in that context, one sees the similarity that every human shares in, that every human is, most significantly, related to God. Honor, power, and glory, chief among the differentia of human persons, no longer seem worth pursuing. Consequently, one no longer takes delight in such things, since to delight in them is to attain them and to think of them as worth the pursuit. When one no longer delights in them, then he also no longer delights in the differences they mark between oneself and others. One focuses one's attention on the deep similarities instead. Seeing others within the context of those similarities, the reader is now able to take joy[97] in the differences of his neighbor, a feature that before had been, for example, the object of his envy.[98]

In another key set of passages, Kierkegaard relates love to the emotions. He writes, "Love is a passion of the emotions, but in this emotion a person, even before he relates to the objects of love, should first relate to God...."[99] Love may be termed an emotion because love as a passion is the basis for a wide variety of construals of oneself and others. Based on a concern for one's neighbor that arises within a concern for one's relation to God, the loving person is bound to the neighbor through a range of appropriate emotions.[100] What particular emotions count as proper in differing circumstances

[97] See ibid., 80.

[98] See ibid., 80–81.

[99] Ibid., 112.

[100] "Your friend, your beloved, your child, or whoever is an object of your love has a claim upon an expression of [your emotion] also in words if it actually moves you inwardly. The emotion is not your possession but belongs to the other; the expression is your debt to him, since *in the emotion you belong to him who moves you and you become aware that you belong to him*" (Kierkegaard, *Works of Love*, 12, emphasis added).

depends, of course, on how those circumstances impinge on the concern at the base of the emotion.

Later in the fourth deliberation, Kierkegaard gives an example that demonstrates the importance of right emotion and the way in which concepts shape it. He imagines a rich person who, motivated by Christian love, provides a meal for the poor and lowly. Christian love also requires, says Kierkegaard, that the benefactor call the meal a "banquet." He insists on this "language usage" because "the one who feeds the poor—but still has not been victorious over his mind in such a way that he calls this meal a banquet—sees the poor and the lowly only as the poor and the lowly. The one who gives *the banquet* sees the neighbor in the poor and the lowly—however ludicrous this may seem in the eyes of the world."[101] In a draft, Kierkegaard notes that a "district clerk or a relief officer" may also provide a meal for the poor. So the distinguishing mark of Christian love is not merely to provide a meal but to do so and call it a banquet, an occasion of joy and delight. The work of love described in this passage is essentially a matter of vision. The Christian "language usage" reveals the benefactor's perception. He "sees" the poor as his neighbors, and his vision reveals itself in the joy with which he feasts with them. Christian love is a matter of perception with the eyes of a properly formed heart, rather than with the "eyes of the world."

By calling his meal with the poor a banquet, the rich man betrays the joy and excitement inseparable from his vision of them as neighbors feasting together. Just these emotions, these perceptions of the poor, scandalize his peers. The scandal, proximately caused by the rich man's terminology, reveals deep-seated differences in the concepts shaping the rich man's

---

[101] Kierkegaard, *Works of Love*, 83.

emotions and his peers'. The difference in terminology reveals a difference in perception because emotions, taken as concern-based construals, are shaped by thoughts expressed in language.[102] In a later journal entry, Kierkegaard observes that Christianity has its own language, "different from all human language," having "the qualitative difference of a difference of concept."[103] He illustrates the difference with the terms "loss" and "gain." "For example, Christianity says that to lose the earthly is a gain, that to possess it is a loss." When the rich man sees his use of resources and his peers' reaction to his eccentric endeavors, he will see it *as* loss or gain. As his peers understand those concepts, the rich man can only be suffering loss. But to see his mealtime fellowship with the poor and lowly as a loss is not to see his guests Christianly, as his neighbors. Consequently, the rich man needs to clarify the concepts of loss and gain in relation to his faith. If he has done so, and he grasps the Christian inversion of "loss" and "gain," relative to the worldly use of those concepts, he will see his mealtime fellowship, and the depletion of his resources and reputation, as a gain. It will then be natural to call the meal a banquet and to engage in it with joy and enthusiasm and gratitude. The emotions based on the concern for one's neighbor will take their shape from the way in which one understands concepts like "neighbor" and "banquet." Central to the exercise of Christian love in this example is the ability to make conceptual distinctions that depend on language, and so to use language appropriately. In much of *Works of Love*, Kierkegaard guides the reader through the necessary conceptual distinctions and schools him in the proper use of

---

[102] Roberts, "Dialectical Emotions," 89.
[103] Kierkegaard, *Journals*, 2:2333.

language, so that he can see accurately with the eyes of the heart.

Love, Authority, and the Law

In the first three deliberations of *Works of Love,* Kierkegaard undoes the tangled mess of the reader's self-deceptions by revealing the inadequacies of self-love. He does so mostly from an internal perspective, arguing, for example, that self-love is unstable and tends to change, despite its own desire to be lasting. Sometimes he argues from features of self-love that prove unacceptable to a Christian point of view, pointing, for example, to its inherent self-deception. But this tactic is also internal to the implied reader's own perspective, given the reader's understanding of himself as Christian. By the time the implied reader comes to the fourth deliberation, he is ready to admit the inadequacy of his current condition and willing to see what true Christian love really is. The fourth deliberation then clarifies the nature of Christian love. With a better grasp of the concepts, the reader may think himself ready to begin the process of acquiring Christian love.

The fifth deliberation opens with a caution about beginning with a promise, since a promise puts distance between the one who promises and that which he promises. Rather than beginning with good intentions for his own chosen *ascesis,* the deliberation places the reader in conversation with the Law. Kierkegaard recounts a story from the life of Christ about a conversation with a Pharisee concerning the Law and one's neighbor. This story brings the reader to realize that the beginning of his love is not the beginning of a story of self-improvement. Instead, the beginning of his love is part of a story of response to the divine initiative in the Law and in Christ, the fulfillment of the Law. The Law makes it possible for the reader to begin to love by making him aware of the story in which he already plays his role and by showing him how that story can continue. The Law introduces the reader to his guilt, proposes a new but indefinite future for the continuation of his story, reveals the reader's inability, and provides a limiting context for the reader's moral vision, remedying the dizziness in which he began.

One cannot begin to love by promising to love because the promise introduces distance between the one who promises and the actual works of love. One who promises can relate to love wishfully, dreamily, curiously, or in myriad other ways that provide an escape from, or a delay in, beginning the activities of love. The one who promises may, for instance, want to dwell on the question, "What is love?" This question makes the promising one seem responsible—after all, one should not promise what one does not even understand—but prevents one from engaging in the works of love, as one's curiosity idles in speculation. Kierkegaard notes that the Apostle Paul addresses the question, not by supplying a possible speculative definition of love, but by referring the reader to the Law. Kierkegaard takes as his text Paul's assertion that "love is the fulfilling of the law." The fifth deliberation forestalls delaying tactics by forcefully reminding the reader of the Law and its authority.

Kierkegaard is somewhat ambiguous in his references to "the Law." The apostle's claim that love is the fulfilling of the law arguably refers, in context, to the Mosaic Law, and especially the Decalogue.[104] On the other hand, "the Law" also refers to Christ's command, reiterating a Mosaic injunction, "You shall love your neighbor as yourself."[105] Since Christ

[104] Romans 13:8–10.

[105] See Matthew 22:39 and Luke 10:27–29; and *Works of Love*, 17, 96.

gives his command as a summary of the Mosaic Law, this ambiguity is not, perhaps, too confusing. But Kierkegaard also suggests that "the Law" includes its infinite specifications, its endless particular requirements.[106] One commentator has argued that "the Law" in *Works of Love* also refers to "rational, universal standards of ethical conduct" in an "Enlightenment philosophical sense." This commentator even insists that Kierkegaard's use of the Law "indicates that what Moses was to St. Paul, Kant can be to us."[107]

But the Law's usefulness in compelling the reader to begin the life of Christian love—a life he has now come to see as desirable—rests on the authority of the Lawgiver, an authority Kant does not possess. Moving from Paul to Christ, Kierkegaard recounts the story in which Christ's interlocutor responds to his command that one love one's neighbor by asking, "Who is my neighbor?" The interlocutor wished to escape from the responsibility of love by engaging Christ in a speculative debate. But Christ cuts through the dialectics with "divine authority." His authority "imprisons" the questioner "in the task" or "assign[s] the task." As the reader puts himself in the place of the questioner, he sees that Christ's authority is essential to the reader's beginning the task of loving. Kierkegaard further insists that it is Christ's personal authority as the God-Man that makes the difference. He writes, "[I]t is infinitely important that it is Christ who has said it, and when it is told to the single individual it is to *him* that it is told."[108]

Why should authority, and particularly Christ's personal authority, make such a difference here? Kierkegaard suggests two reasons. First, one must remember that the reader, though

[106] Kierkegaard, *Works of Love*, 105–106.
[107] Kirmmse, *Kierkegaard*, 309.
[108] Kierkegaard, *Works of Love*, 97.

newly aware of his self-deception, still suffers from self-division. Consequently, the reader is prone to "busyness."

> To be busy is to occupy oneself, divided and scattered (which follows from the object that occupies one), with all the multiplicity in which it is simply impossible for a person to be whole, whole in all of it or whole in any particular part of it, something only the insane can succeed in doing. To be busy is, divided and scattered, to occupy oneself with what makes a person divided and scattered. But Christian love, which is the fulfilling of the Law, is, whole and collected, present in its every expression, and yet it is sheer action; consequently it is as far from inaction as it is from busyness.[109]

The reader, divided among competing drives and inclinations, is ready to busy himself with the business of love. But because the reader is essentially divided, no matter how much he wishes to become loving, he cannot set that task for himself. Any task he sets himself on the basis of some drive or inclination competes with others. And any task set purely in thought will lack the passion to become actual. He cannot be wholly present in any of them, since he must busily step back from all of them to question them, debate them, and demonstrate their necessity. That distance then prevents the self from acting decisively on them. Loving Christianly, on the other hand, is not a matter of balancing drives and inclinations but of situating all of them within one's fundamental, and mutually implicating, concerns for one's God-relation and one's neighbor. So the task of Christian love cannot be set for the divided self by the divided self. Loving Christianly requires a unity of the self. Consequently, it can only be assigned by a source external to the self. Since authority is, on Kierkegaard's

---

[109] Ibid., 98.

view, "to assign the task," Christian love requires an authority external to the self.[110]

Second, the authority must be divine and it must be personal. In *Upbuilding Discourses in Various Spirits*, Kierkegaard anticipates the assumptions about authority behind *Works of Love*.[111] He describes the comparative disadvantage adults suffer in relation to children in completing some task. "The difficulty for the adult...is that he must do double work: work to find out the task and get it firmly set and then work to carry out the task. The greatest difficulty seems to be just to get the task firmly set or actually to get set firmly on what the task is."[112] Children avoid this problem because of their parents' authority to set the task for them. Adults, on the other hand, are their own authorities, both masters and servants of themselves. This "difficult situation" quickly deteriorates when the adult must begin a task, especially the moral one: "instead of becoming his own master a person becomes unstable, irresolute, vacillating; he runs from one thing to the other, tears down and builds up and begins again from the beginning." Trapped in "busy trifling deliberation or in fruitless wishing," " he uses much time, much diligence, and much energy, and it is all as good as wasted, because the task does not remain fixed, because there is no master, since he, of course, should be his own master."[113] Because children have

---

110 Merold Westphal makes a related and perceptive point: "[T]he attempt to put the pathological in its place [through self-legislation] came across as a noble resistance to self-love. Now it turns out to be but the flip side of a dual attempt to keep the self unconditionally in charge." See "Commanded Love and Moral Autonomy: The Kierkegaard-Habermas Debate," *Kierkegaard Studies: Yearbook* (January 1998): 6.

111 See also Judge William's story of his father's authority in Kierkegaard, *Either/Or*, 2:268–69.

112 Kierkegaard, *Upbuilding Discourses*, 294.

113 Ibid., 295.

parents to set the task for them, they can begin immediately. Adults, essentially equal to one another, have only themselves or God to set the task.[114] If they are to make a good beginning, argues Kierkegaard, they must depend on divine authority.

Kierkegaard imagines some alternatives to divine authority in *Works of Love,* alternatives that promise to provide adults with a purely human authority yet without sacrificing their essential equality. He briefly presents possibilities recognizable as Kantian or contractarian, only to dismiss them.[115] His criticisms are not, however, obviously trenchant. With respect to contractarian theories, for instance, he asserts first that a universal assembly for contract negotiations could never occur, especially since the dead could not be included. That criticism also implies a second: a purely hypothetical contract would fail to provide the authority the reader needs to begin. Next, he denies that a universal assembly could ever come to any consensus. Finally, if no consensus is available, the agreement's provisions must be determined by a majority vote, but deciding how much of a majority is an exercise in complete arbitrariness.

Some commentators have taken these reflections as straightforward criticisms of the theories in question, meant to demonstrate the superiority of Kierkegaard's own competing theory.[116] But that reading faces several objections. First, nothing in the deliberations has indicated that Kierkegaard's implied reader is especially conversant with contemporary moral theories. Even more significantly, because the reader already has Christian commitments, he already admits God's

---

[114] See Kierkegaard, *Works of Love,* 189–190, for an analogy comparing parental and divine authority.

[115] Kierkegaard, *Works of Love,* 115–17.

[116] See C. Stephen Evans, "Authority and Transcendence in *Works of Love,*" *Kierkegaard Studies: Yearkbook* (January 1998): 25–30.

authority in morality. Second, Kierkegaard's criticisms are not particularly compelling. Indeed, they are, for the most part, the stock responses to these moral theories as taught in any sophomore-level ethics class. Sophisticated proponents of these theories have more than one way to rebut Kierkegaard's criticisms. For example, Jurgen Habermas's analysis of the normative conditions for communication does not rely on a merely pretend agreement and makes strong arguments for a universal consensus on the norms he proposes.[117]

If Kierkegaard's criticisms are not sophisticated enough to demonstrate the invalidity of, for example, contractarian moral theory, then why does he make them? The answer to this question provides the third reason to reject Kierkegaard's comments about Kantianism and contractarianism as a piece of straightforward moral theorizing by suggesting a more plausible interpretation. Kierkegaard chooses such obvious criticisms to prompt the reader, once more, to see himself in the text. These are just the sorts of quibbles the reader himself would bring, once he seeks refuge in theoretical debate. And they demonstrate that the fundamental problem with the reader is not a theoretical or speculative problem but a condition of "mutiny" or "rebellion" against divine authority. The important point is not the ways in which human authority fails as an ultimate source of moral authority. The point is that the reader's resort to theoretical disputes about the issue is no more than an occasion of culpable evasion, delaying, and busyness that prevents him from immediately beginning the task he knows God has assigned. Kierkegaard's final criticism of contractarianism makes just this point explicit. If a

---

[117] See, for instance, William Rehg, S.J., *Insight and Solidarity: The Discourse Ethics of Jurgen Habermas* (Los Angeles: University of California Press, 1994) 147–48.

consensus of interested parties sets the moral task, then I must learn what it is from the others. But the others too learn the task from others, and so on in an infinite deferral of actually beginning. Whether the others are other real humans, other imagined humans, or other parts of myself, depending on them to set the moral task is always a matter of delay. Only a divine authority that stands over against all the others—including myself—can set the task without stimulating the busyness that derails. Perhaps a dim recognition of this fact explains Kant's insistence that I must hear the law I legislate for myself as if it were a divine command and Hobbes's celebration of the Leviathan created by social contract as a mortal god.

The authority must be personal, that is, it must be Christ who commands, because in Christ is the Absolute Paradox, the eternal in time, that makes it possible for humans to be contemporaneous with the Divine. If the command were not Christ's command, it would not be Christian love. Kierkegaard writes, "Our text is the *apostolic* word, we are speaking about *Christian love*; therefore here the law can be only *God's Law*."[118] It must be personal also because it is the reader who hears. All along, Kierkegaard has depended on the reader's being a Christian, a person of faith, though needing to become a Christian in a deeper sense. This reader's faith, insofar as it is genuine Christian faith at all, is an interest in his relationship with the God-Man, Jesus Christ, so that he construes Christ as deserving of grateful obedience. Hence, because the command comes from Christ, it carries with it the divine authority it needs and it connects to the passions that make the reader

[118] Kierkegaard, *Works of Love*, 106.

capable of recognizing it.[119] The reader can hear Christ's command as authoritative because of his faith.[120]

These remarks about the importance of Christ's personal authority to Kierkegaard's pedagogy show well enough why "the Law" in *Works of Love* cannot refer in any direct way to the Enlightenment notion of a universal, rational law whose authority derives from each individual's own reason or from each individual's own consent to a hypothetical or actual contract. Kierkegaard's implied reader is not the Enlightenment's ideal of a rational agent emancipated from tradition and external authority.[121] Kierkegaard's reader is essentially committed through faith to a relationship with God that binds his heart without limit, though Kierkegaard has to make him aware of the many ways in which he self-deceptively attempts to emancipate himself from those bonds.[122] The Law has its force within the context of faith. Someone without faith, employing only reason, would hear the royal Law not as authoritative, compelling one to begin the task, but as mere possibility, to be investigated, questioned, criticized, and otherwise made an object of speculation.

Kierkegaard suggests three explicit comparisons between the Law and love to clarify its proper role in the reader's transition to Christian love. The Law is to love as a shadow is to an object it precedes; as an artist's preliminary sketch is to

---

[119] See Kierkegaard, *Journals*, 3:2377: "[A]uthority is related to pathos.... If there is a question about an authority, then the issue is one of authority—ergo, it can be contested neither objectively nor anonymously. I must be contemporary with it, and in my own private person go to Christ and say: You are a deceiver."

[120] See Stephen Dunning, "Who Sets the Task: Kierkegaard on Authority," in *Foundations of Kierkegaard's Vision of Community*, ed. George B. Connell and C. Stephen Evans (Atlantic Highlands NJ: Humanities Press, 1992) 18–32.

[121] Kierkegaard, *Works of Love*, 114–15.

[122] Ibid., 148.

the finished painting; and as understanding is to faith.[123] These three metaphors illustrate three truths about the relationship between the Law and love. First, the Law is somehow weaker, less substantial than love, just as a shadow is weaker and less substantial than the object it precedes. Second, the Law is an indefinite plan and love is the definite execution of that plan, just as the sketch finds its finality in the painting. Third, the Law works by multiplying demands in infinitely increasing specificity and precision but never arrives at love, whereas love works by decisively acting. In the same way, the understanding endlessly calculates ever-changing probabilities without ever coming to certainty, but faith finds certainty by decisively stepping out in belief. Finally, just as there is no final conflict between the sketch and the painting or between understanding's attempts to find certainty and faith's decisive movements, so there is no final conflict between the Law and love. Of course, that lack of conflict obtains only when the two are rightly ordered. Someone who absolutely prefers sketching to painting or understanding to believing produces a conflict where none need be. And the same holds for the Law and love as well.

Kierkegaard goes even further. So far is the Law from conflict with love that love is the fulfilling of the Law. Love makes the Law definite and ends its perpetually ramifying specifications, making the active works of love possible. Following the Apostle Paul, Kierkegaard explains, "Christ was the end of the Law."[124] Just as the finished painting is the reason for the sketches and the reason to end the sketching, so Christ is the both the "perfection" and the "downfall" of the

---

[123] Ibid., 104–105.
[124] Ibid., 99.

Law. To show how love fulfills the Law, Kierkegaard directs the reader's attention to Christ, who is its end.

Christ "was Love, and his love was the fulfilling of the Law."[125] Consequently, Christ is the example or prototype for the reader who wants to learn to love Christianly.[126] Kierkegaard provides a fairly lengthy meditation on the life of Christ. Christ's life establishes a concrete pattern of love that can provide a limit capable of rescuing the reader from the dizziness implied by the Law.[127] Christ's life reveals a new kind of collision or conflict stemming from a new kind of love. Previously, humans had only considered the conflicts between self-love and the various circumstances that threaten to frustrate it. But Christ's story also reveals a more essential kind of collision, one between different conceptions of love. The worldly conception of love sees it as a relation between two in which they attempt to negotiate the satisfaction of their own drives and inclinations. The Christian conception of love presents it as a relation between three, between two humans with God as the middle term. Christian love aims to help the beloved love God more; it turns the beloved not toward itself but toward God. Kierkegaard gives examples from the life of Christ and his relationships with Mary, Peter, and the disciples. Christ's love was always active in work and prayer, both rebuked and forgave, made no demands on others merely for his own benefit, never compromised, and did not give itself even to his own family in exclusion of others.[128] However, if the beloved does not want to turn toward God, Christian love runs

---

[125] Ibid.

[126] Kierkegaard, *Journals*, 2:1837; Kierkegaard, *Works of Love*, 471, 288.

[127] Kierkegaard, *Works of Love*, 105: "[T]he concept of the Law is to be inexhaustible, limitless, endless in its provisions; every provision begets of itself an even more precise provision, and in turn a still more precise provision by reference in relation to the new provision, and so on infinitely."

[128] Kierkegaard, *Works of Love*, 100.

the risk of appearing as hate to its objects. In Christ's story, the result was crucifixion. The conflict between different conceptions of love becomes a collision between Christ and the world.

By concretely and perfectly exemplifying the demands of the Law in his life, Christ provides definition to the Law and a model for imitation. The reader apprehends Christ's life in this respect as providing new possibilities for the continuation of his own story. Kierkegaard more or less directly pictures the reader's future for him. Consider these two passages:

> [W]e dare not assent to the superficial talk that if a person really has love people will then also love him. He will more likely be accused of self-love just because he will not love people in the sense in which they, self-forgiving, love themselves. ...Yet the one who fights the good fight to express that God exists and is the Lord whose explanation is to be obeyed unconditionally is fighting for God.[129]

> [I]f in loving you are unwilling to be a traitor either to God or to yourself or to the others, you will have to put up with being called self-loving. Your friend will very likely not care for your conviction that truly to love yourself is to love God, that to love another human being is to help him love God.[130]

Kierkegaard begins with the Law, finds its definition in the life of Christ, and then pictures for the reader a future modeled on Christ's life, a future of conflict between the reader as one who loves Christianly and those whose conception of love is worldly. That is to say, Kierkegaard employs the Law, understood Christianly, to alter his reader's self-interpretive narrative. The conflicts and resolutions in terms of which the reader sees his life before his encounter with Christ as the

---

[129] Ibid., 120.
[130] Ibid., 127.

fulfilling of the Law are conflicts between his love and its external obstacles. But now he comes to see the possibility of a new continuation to his story, one in which the conflicts are between conceptions of love and in which the resolutions usually entail his own suffering.

As prototype, Christ fulfills the indefiniteness of the Law. But at the same time, his existence as prototype also reinforces the rigors of the Law. The reader who takes Christ as his prototype, and so pays attention to the demands of the Law that Christ's life perfectly fulfills, will become more aware of the self-deception under which he usually labors and that enables him to convince himself of the genuineness of his love. Furthermore, as Kierkegaard focuses the reader's attention on the possible continuations of his story, he will realize that not only is a future of perfect conformity to the prototype beyond his powers but also that his past is already an unfulfilled possibility, that the future he can now imagine could have been his past, were it not for his rebellion and self-deception. Consequently, the reader now faces an even more insurmountable obstacle in the way of beginning to love, since his past stands as a waste of time that he cannot redeem. Kirmmse rightly sums up this aspect of the Law by observing, "The Law is a preparatory stage whose function is to show us that it does not admit of human fulfillment."[131] The Law exacts a "groan" from the reader because it demands more than he can bear in his disordered state, even—or especially—when the Law is seen as fulfilled in Christ's life of love. Since the authority behind the Law is Christ's personal and divine

[131] Kirmmse, *Kierkegaard*, 309. Two caveats are in order. First, this function is not the Law's only function, as can be seen from the fact that Christ as the fulfilling of the Law is proposed as a model of imitation. Second, Christ fulfilled the law precisely in his human nature, so that "human" in Kirmmse's formula should read instead "sinful human."

authority, the reader must come to see himself as guilty, not just of moral failure, but also of sin.[132]

Christ's fulfilling of the Law as a prototype does not, then, lessen the rigors or demands of the Law. But Christ's fulfilling of the Law in another way does remedy the reader's problem, though without weakening the Law. Christ's life brought "the sacrifice of atonement."[133] Atonement is a repetition: "God loved us first; and again the second time, when it was a matter of the Atonement, God was the one who came first—although in the sense of justice he was the one who had the furthest to come."[134] By virtue of the atonement, God forgives the reader his sin and always makes possible a new beginning. In the conclusion to the book, the reader learns that he is not left alone in this new beginning. God becomes his co-worker, though this assistance is itself a kind of difficulty. "The difficulty, therefore, is just that I am to work together with him, if not in any other way, then through the continual understanding that I am able to do nothing at all, something that is not understood once and for all."[135] Denying his own self-sufficiency and relying on the infinite power of God becomes the reader's task. In beginning this task, he begins to love.

The Reader's Repetition of Ordinary Loves

Does Christian Love Replace Ordinary Loves? I have claimed that the narrative of *Works of Love* is a narrative of repetition, not of replacement. But hasn't Christian love replaced all other loves for the reader? It might appear that Christian love differs so

---

[132] Kierkegaard, *Works of Love*, 104, 133–34.
[133] Ibid., 112.
[134] Ibid., 336. See also Mooney, "*Repetition*," 297–99.
[135] Kierkegaard, *Works of Love*, 363.

completely from the love of friend, wife, and countryman that the reader has simply lost the loves with which he started. Kierkegaard himself anticipates this reading when he writes, "Frequently, although in different ways,...the objection is made against Christianity that it displaces erotic love and friendship."[136] The contemporary literature abounds in such objections to Kierkegaard's depiction of Christian love, and many passages can be adduced in its favor.

First, Kierkegaard early and often reduces ordinary loves to selfishness. I have argued that the selfishness of "preferential" loves is due to their roots in a divided self. Nevertheless, his denunciation of preferential loves, especially but not exclusively in the early sections, may suggest to some a stronger thesis. Perhaps Kierkegaard means to say not only that every love proceeding from a divided self must prove arbitrary and unstable, but also that every ordinary kind of love does in fact proceed from a divided self. Furthermore, he sometimes presents Christian love as blind to the differences that make one person stand out from among others.[137] But ordinary loves are attentive to just those particulars to which neighbor love seems blind. To love one's wife as one's wife requires paying attention to all those characteristics that differentiate her from all the other women in the world and to valuing her more than all the others. So loving Christianly seems to replace loving in any ordinary way because of the partiality Christian love rejects and ordinary loves assume.

Second, the natural loves require mutuality. They find their characteristic joy in love returned and their characteristic melancholy in unrequited love. But neighbor love suffers no change when it is not reciprocated, as Kierkegaard implies in

---

[136] Ibid., 44.
[137] See, for example, ibid. 68.

several key passages. For example, early in the book, he suggests that someone on a desert island could love Christianly.[138] Similarly, towards the end of the second series of deliberations, he compares Christian love to love for the dead.[139] But to love someone as one dead is not to engage the other in a genuinely intersubjective exchange. Loving Christianly seems to secure stability and tranquility at the cost of the vulnerabilities implied by true mutuality.

Finally, the ordinary loves exhibit a deep concern for the life and material well-being of their objects. Kierkegaard's description of Christian love suggests that it does not. Christian love has as its chief concern building up the neighbor in the love of God. But material resources are not, apparently, very important for loving God. For instance, Kierkegaard goes to some lengths to show that the poor as well as the rich can equally engage in mercifulness as a work of love.[140] But if the poor can engage in works of love while remaining poor, then a love aimed at helping others in the works of love has no incentive for relieving poverty and need. Loving Christianly, one might think, depends on a spiritual equality that denies the need for attention to material well-being.

Commentators have frequently noted these three points, often suggesting that common moral intuitions land on the side of ordinary love in all these cases. Consequently, they insist that Kierkegaard's ideal of Christian love fails to be compelling. Capable interpreters have cogently defended *Works of Love* on each count, and I refer the reader to some of their arguments.[141] Kierkegaard's defenders have

[138] Kierkegaard, ibid., 68.

[139] Kierkegaard, ibid., 345-58.

[140] Kierkegaard, ibid., 315-30.

[141] See Louise Carroll Keeley's "Subjectivity and World in *Works of Love*," in *Foundations of Kierkegaard's Vision of Community*, ed. Connell and Evans, 96–

demonstrated that Christian love is not as objectionably blind to particulars, mutuality, and material well-being as might at first appear. Though they have produced many fine and valuable studies, they sometimes create a misleading impression by appearing to root for Christian love in a competition against the others. In defense of Kierkegaard, they record a dialectical victory for Christian love in the contest, because it remedies the defects of its rivals without losing the best in the ordinary loves.

But just as Kierkegaard refused to countenance any human defense of Christian faith because such a defense makes faith one option, even if the best, among many essentially similar alternatives, so I believe his defenders should be wary about apologetics for Christian love that reduce it to one alternative among many kinds of love or one species of a genus of virtue. After raising the basic objection noted above, Kierkegaard identifies the dangers attendant on "defending" Christianity. Rather than defending Christianity by comparing its love with others, Kierkegaard believes that one should make clear the issue Christianity insists on, so that "the single individual" can choose how to respond. Christian love is not one love among many nor one virtue among many, but the contextualizing vision that provides the proper setting for the various loves and virtues. Christian love displaces more

108; Lee Barret's "The Neighbor's Material and Social Well-Being in Kierkegaard's *Works of Love*: Does it Matter?"; M. J. Ferreira's "Mutual Responsiveness in Relation: The Challenge of the Ninth Deliberation"; and Louise Carroll Keeley's "Loving 'No One,' Loving Everyone: The Work of Love in Recollecting One Dead in Kierkegaard's *Works of Love*," all in *International Kierkegaard Commentary: Works of Love*, ed. Robert L. Perkins (Macon GA: Mercer University Press, 1999); and Ferreira's "Equality, Impartiality, and Moral Blindness in Kierkegaard's *Works of Love*," *Journal of Religious Ethics* 25/1 (Spring 1997): 65–85, as well as her *Love's Grateful Striving: A Commentary on Kierkegaard's* Works of Love (New York: Oxford University Press, 2001).

ordinary loves by replacing them on the "throne" of the heart, not by eliminating them all together.[142]

The Distinctiveness of Christian Love. I have suggested already that Christian love is a peculiar sort of virtue. Properly speaking, however, Christian love is not quite a virtue but a kind of analogue of the virtues. Like many of them, as noted above, Christian love is a stable quality of character disposing its possessor to a range of perceptions related to a fundamental concern and so to a range of emotions. But Kierkegaard denies that Christian love is "related as a type to other types of love."[143] Instead, Christian love provides the context in which the other loves find their place and meaning. The corollary of this argument, of course, is that Christian love is also not a species of a genus of virtue, but instead a context in which all other virtues assume a deeper meaning. The best defense of Kierkegaard against the criticisms articulated above does not so much show that Christian love better exemplifies partiality, mutuality, and material concern, but that Christian love constitutes the context in terms of which partiality, mutuality, and material concern become meaningful. And the corollary also holds: if material concern is perfected by the virtue of compassion, then Christian love does not feel with other needs more than compassion, but gives compassion its deepest meaning and significance.

A distinction Kierkegaard makes in *Works of Love* may sharpen these claims. Kierkegaard calls Christian love a "being-for-others" quality, distinguishing it from "being-for-itself' qualities. The latter are qualities that require a self-understanding according to which one sees oneself in the context of an ideal. To be wise, for example, one must

---

[142] Kierkegaard, *Works of Love*, 44. See also *Upbuilding Discourses*, 129.
[143] Kierkegaard, *Works of Love*, 66.

understand and evaluate oneself in relation to an ideal of wisdom. Someone with no concern for wisdom could only be wise by accident, and accidental wisdom is not what one usually means by the term "wise." But possessing the quality of wisdom implies nothing about one's understanding of others in their relation to wisdom. Benevolence as a virtue has the same structure. Despite its desire to do well to others, even all others, benevolence does not assume that its objects are themselves benevolent. As a being-for-others quality, by contrast, love is essentially an understanding of oneself and others in light of everyone's relation to God such that one sees others as also possessing love. The loving person never doubts the love that exists in another as a ground or foundation, since every person is equally related to God who is love.[144] Kierkegaard writes that love is thus "a quality by which or in which you are for others."[145]

This claim makes Christian love sound like a relationship. Like friendship, Christian love is a relation with others that creates an arena for the exercise of the various virtues. The second series of deliberations accordingly describes many different virtues, such as mercifulness and perseverance that gain their greatest significance in the context created by Christian love. Christian love unites these other virtues not by reducing them to some single disposition but by giving them their point and purpose in the context of a relationship. Unlike friendship, however, which requires reciprocity, Christian love sees the other in light of the other's relation to a third, God. By virtue of the divine middle term, Christian love sustains a relation to the neighbor that does not require reciprocity. So

---

[144] See the deliberation "Love Builds Up," especially Kierkegaard, *Works of Love*, 219.

[145] Kierkegaard, *Works of Love*, 223.

Christian love is a quality not like benevolence, but not quite like friendship either.

Opposing Christian love to friendship or to compassion without qualification, then, ultimately misleads, because it implies that Christian love is a relationship or quality like those. But Kierkegaard's fundamental point is that Christian love is not one more rival for the heart's deepest concern or one more virtue perfecting the self. Instead, it is an entirely different kind of quality, one that can provide significance to the others. Consider the following passage:

> If one were to state and describe in a single sentence the victory Christianity has won over the world or, even more correctly, the victory by which it has more than overcome the world (since Christianity has never wanted to conquer in a worldly way), infinity's change that Christianity has as its aim, by which everything indeed remains as it was (since Christianity has never been a friend of the trumpery of novelty) and yet in the sense of infinity has become completely new—then I know of nothing shorter but also nothing more decisive than this: it has made every human relationship between person and person a relationship of conscience.[146]

Kierkegaard asserts here that Christian love makes ordinary loves new without replacing them by setting them in the most comprehensive context ("infinity"). That context is the relation between the person and God, as one becomes aware of it in conscience. Conscience itself is a knowing with or before God,[147] so that to make every personal relationship a matter of conscience is to make God the middle term in every love. Christian love in this passage is not a love that replaces natural loves but the context that relativizes them.

---

[146] Ibid., 135.

[147] Kierkegaard, *Journals*, 1:683.

In another passage, Kierkegaard attempts to describe more fully what a renewed ordinary love looks like.

> This is Christianity. It is so far from being a matter of first having to get busy to find the beloved that, on the contrary, in loving the beloved we are first to love the neighbor. To drives and inclinations this is no doubt a strange, chilling inversion; yet it is Christianity and no more chilling than the spirit is in relation to the sensate or the sensate-psychical; moreover, it is specifically a quality of the spirit to burn without blazing. Your wife must first and foremost be to you the neighbor; that she is your wife is then a more precise specification of your particular relationship to each other. But what is the eternal foundation must also be the foundation of every expression of the particular.[148]

A person who loves Christianly sees his wife's significance in light of her relation to God and presupposes love in her. But that does not entail ceasing to love her as his wife because those two loves are not in competition, once Christian love is understood correctly. Instead, within the context set by Christian love, he loves her specifically, and with suitable partiality, as his wife. The task of Christian love, Kierkegaard writes, is to find the "once given or chosen object lovable."[149] In other words, to choose a person to love in particular, as spouses do, is not to violate Christian love. But to commit oneself in a particular love and then to cease to see that person lovingly is to violate Christian love. Christian love urges one to love according to particular commitments even at the price of self-denial.[150] The reader continues to love his wife in a way he loves no one else, and the same for his friends and

---

[148] Kierkegaard, *Works of Love*, 141.
[149] Ibid., 166.
[150] Ibid., 55.

fellow citizens: "The beloved, the friend, is of course a human being also in the more ordinary sense and exists as such for the rest of us, but he should exist essentially only as the beloved if you are to fulfill the duty of loving the person you see."[151] Nonetheless, he sees that the most significant thing about them is that they are his neighbors, not that they fulfill a need of the self, even if they do that as well. In this regard, the test of Christian love is not the tenuousness of one's commitments to particular persons, but one's faithfulness to commitments one has already made. When the one who loves Christianly loses the particular love of a spouse, the Christian lover continues to love, continues to relate to the spouse with God as the middle term. The second series of deliberations specifies just what that means: engaging in works of mercy, upbuilding, hope, and so on for the unfaithful spouse. One who can continue to love a chosen or given person in this way, even when that person rejects and reviles one, is one who loves Christianly. At the end of the story, then, the reader does have a genuine repetition. He receives again the particular loves he had thought were lost in the collision with authentically Christian concepts, but now invested with a deeper and more stable significance.

---

[151] Ibid., 165.

5

Kierkegaard and the Limits of Narrative

Throughout his *Four Quartets,* T. S. Eliot reflects on the dynamic patterns that give meaning to the scattered and always receding moments of our lives. Towards the end of "East Coker," he describes that pattern in these words:

> Not the intense moment
> Isolated, with no before and after,
> but a lifetime burning in every moment.
> ....
> There is a time for the evening under starlight,
> A time for the evening under lamplight
> (The evening with the photograph album).[1]

These lines suggest that the sense of a human life emerges, not from an isolated moment of ecstatic rapture or spectacular achievement, but from the pattern implicit in the succession of ordinary moments, illuminating each one from within.

Among philosophers today, many would resonate with Eliot's poetic vision and articulate it in terms of the importance of narrative for human agency and self-understanding. In *After Virtue,* Alasdair MacIntyre argued that the narrative form is a necessary antidote for the atomistic accounts of human action common to the analytic and existentialist traditions. Many philosophers have since followed his lead, and the significance

---

[1] T. S. Eliot, "East Coker," *Four Quartets* (1943; New York: Harcourt Brace & Co., 1971) ll. 192–94, 197–99.

of narrative for personal identity, self-understanding, and ethical reflection has become almost a commonplace. Recently, and perhaps predictably, a growing number of critics have sought to deflate these claims for narrative. These debates have had a special significance for readers of Kierkegaard, many of whom have tried to respond to accusations of irrationalism in Kierkegaard's works by pointing to the MacIntyrean-style emphasis on the narrative unity of a human life that those works make central.

Since my reading of Kierkegaard has focused on his use of narrative and its roots in his fundamental vision of the moral life, these criticisms might seem especially damaging to the present project. So in this chapter, I will engage some of those criticisms and suggest that Kierkegaard's texts themselves point to some limits on the place of narrative in the moral life. I will turn first to some general criticisms of the use of narrative in moral philosophy and then address the limits of narrative as one can find them in Kierkegaard's own thought.

Objections to the Significance of Narratives for Ethics

Personal Identity. Many of those advocating the importance of narrative for ethics have claimed some important connection between narrative and personal identity or between narrative and the unity of the self. MacIntyre, for example, famously declared that the unity of an individual life consists in "the unity of a narrative embodied in a single life" and that "personal identity is just that identity presupposed by the unity of the character which the unity of a narrative requires."[2]

This connection has become an important target for critics of MacIntyre and his allies. Peter Lamarque, for example, writes, "It is far from clear that narrative *produces* unity [of the

---

[2] MacIntyre, *After Virtue*, 218.

self] or personal identity. More plausibly the narrative *presupposes* this unity."[3] Thus, Lamarque takes the narrative concept of selfhood to be a claim about the principle of a person's identity or unity; as Anthony Rudd puts it, he takes MacIntyre to be endowing narrative with a "foundational" role with respect to personal identity.[4] Rudd rightly argues that objections like Lamarque's fail to reach theses like MacIntyre's that claim only that narrative and personal identity are mutually presupposing concepts, rather than that the former somehow brings about the latter.[5] As Rudd puts it, "On the MacIntyrean view that I will defend here, one cannot understand personal identity or ethics without thinking in narrative terms, but narrative itself presupposes protagonists who are persons, and also the making of evaluative judgments."[6]

Like Rudd's argument, the Kierkegaardian argument advanced in this book does not depend on a strong claim about a narrative foundation for personal identity or unity, as critics of narrative approaches to ethics sometimes assume. I would, in fact, demur from such a position even more emphatically than Rudd does, arguing that Kierkegaard is right to reject a quasi-Lockean view of the self sometimes apparently accepted by both sides in the debate over narrative.

Patrick Stokes lucidly identifies the central issue when he points to Locke's "insistence that the identity of the self or person is distinct from both the identity of the body or

[3] Lamarque, "On Not Expecting Too Much from Narrative," 406. Similar criticisms can be found in John Christman, "Narrative Unity as a Condition of Personhood," *Metaphilosophy* 35 (2004): 696–713.

[4] Rudd, "In Defence of Narrative," 60.

[5] MacIntyre, *After Virtue*, 218.

[6] Rudd, "In Defence of Narrative," 61.

organism...*and* the identity of the thinking substance or soul."[7] Locke's heirs thus divide personal or self-identity from the identities of bodies or souls, so that the former depends entirely on one or more psychological criteria. Some of Kierkegaard's friends place him in the Lockean camp. Stokes, for example, argues that Kierkegaard's theory of personal identity can finally solve the conundrums that have long bedeviled Lockeans by making the psychological unity of the self a project to be achieved through taking on responsibility for one's past and future rather than a given feature of the self. In other words, Kierkegaard replaces a descriptive psychological theory with a normative one. Likewise, Rudd suggests that he sees narrative theories of personal identity as on the Lockean side of the divide Stokes has identified. Rudd writes that "both narrative and Lockean accounts are concerned with psychological continuity and thus both give a crucial role to memory," and he finds their difference in the first or third person perspective they take on the relevant memories,[8] not in their focus on the psychological approach. No doubt Rudd does want to distinguish himself from Locke in many important ways, but it is not clear that he is willing to challenge him on the precise point that Stokes emphasizes as essential to the Lockean tradition.[9]

In my view, Stokes and Rudd could both present their cases more clearly and convincingly by more decisively removing themselves from the Lockean problematic. I am not convinced, for example, by Stokes's argument that the Lockean

---

[7] Patrick Stokes, "Locke, Kierkegaard, and the Phenomenology of Personal Identity," *International Journal of Philosophical Studies* 16/5 (2008): 646.

[8] Rudd, "In Defence of Narrative," 435n45.

[9] See Rudd's "Narrative, Expression, and Mental Substance," *Inquiry* 48 (2005): 413–35, for his more developed and nuanced views on the identity issue, including the important role he gives the body.

distinction is mirrored in *Concluding Unscientific Postscript*, in which a "human being in general" is equivalent to Lockean "person-identity" and "inwardness" is equivalent to "the self I affectively identify with."[10] Inwardness is better construed in terms of character,[11] the dispositional make-up of an agent; but the Lockean problematic moves the concept from the field of agency to that of knowing, in this case, knowing oneself. On the other hand, Stokes is right to say that a lack of Lockean self-identity is, for Kierkegaard, a moral failure, a "failure to take responsibility for the past or future."[12] But this point suggests to me that we can achieve more clarity by taking Kierkegaard's insights as criticisms of the Lockean approach rather than as solutions to its problems.

In any case, other parties to the debate about the significance of narrative in ethics more explicitly maintain that the principle of personal identity is the exercise of a mental act. Galen Strawson, for example, describes the self as "that which I now experience myself to be when I'm apprehending myself specifically as an inner mental presence."[13] Christman argues that "What is required for unified personhood is that the subject of that life be a reflecting subject whose self-interpretations make enough sense of those events that a consistent character can be seen at their center."[14] These descriptions of personhood are all variations on Locke's notion, as Rudd recognizes, that a person is a being able "to consider itself as itself."[15]

---

[10] Stokes, "Locke, Kierkegaard," 650.
[11] See Roberts, "Existence, Emotion, and Virtue," 180–82.
[12] Stokes, "Locke, Kierkegaard," 662.
[13] Strawson, "Against Narrativity," 433.
[14] Christman, "Narrative Unity as a Condition of Personhood," 710.
[15] Rudd, "In Defence of Narrative," 61.

A Kierkegaardian account of personhood must surely make a central place for the kind of reflexivity often the focus of Lockean accounts. But the person must also be more than that reflexivity itself or even a capacity for it. As Anti-Climacus has it in *The Sickness Unto Death*, the self is a synthesis that relates itself to itself; and the synthesis is a relation of the given and that which transcends the given.[16] In Anti-Climacus's formula, the self is not defined by psychological criteria, but instead includes the bodily and other given realities that provide reflection with its materials in the first place. To be a person is thus not merely to reflect on oneself in any particular fashion but rather to be endowed with a gift and task that sets one, as an individual, before God. So on this Kierkegaardian view, the narrative mode appears not as the efficient cause or foundation for personal identity but rather as an essential form of self-understanding following on one's receiving one's identity in providential gift and task.

For many contemporary philosophers, on the other hand, the Lockean picture of the self is another attempt to take up a task while denying the gift. As such, it is resistant to the narrative mode, because it begins by eliminating the self's relation to the past that is captured in Kierkegaard's notion of the gift. Unmoored in that way, broadly Lockean intuitions lead to positions like that of Strawson. Strawson identifies some people as "Episodics," experiencing themselves as unconnected to and unconcerned about the past and the future precisely as past and future. Only a Lockean could arrive at such a picture of human selves, but once allow Lockean intuitions and such pictures can easily attain a compelling force. Advocates of narrative as an essential form of moral self-

[16] Kierkegaard, *Sickness Unto Death*, 13.

understanding would, in my opinion, do well to jettison any lingering Lockean sympathies.

Self-Deception. Another common criticism of the use of narrative as a category of moral reflection appeals to the temptation to self-deception. According to John Lippitt, for example, "In asking myself whether my life possesses narrative unity, I shall be waging a perennial battle against self-deception."[17] Likewise, Galen Strawson allows that narrative self-articulation is not necessarily deceptive but insists that it almost always is in fact, relying on certain aspects of the neurophysiology of memory for his evidence.[18] And Phillip Quinn argues that any narrative self-understanding must be "haunted" by the fear that the stories we tell about our lives "will turn out to be almost entirely a retrospective illusion."[19]

Such critics tend to invest the phenomenon of self-deception with a great deal of significance, suggesting that it entirely deflates the usefulness of appeals to narrative self-understanding. Since one is tempted to tell false stories about oneself, they imply, no story one tells can be believed. But no such momentous conclusions follow from the rather obvious fact that, when we attempt to understand ourselves in moral terms, we are tempted to self-deception. Rudd, for example, rightly responds to these criticisms by pointing out that narrative self-understandings can, of course, be revised.[20] So to

---

[17] Lippitt, "Getting the Story Straight," 50. Lamarque makes a similar point; see Lamarque, "On Not Expecting Too Much from Narrative," 406.

[18] Strawson, "Against Narrativity," 443, 447. James Battersby briefly replies to Strawson's neurophysiological evidence; see his "Narrativity, Self, and Self-Representation," *Narrative* 14 (2006): 44n3.

[19] Philip L. Quinn, "Unity and Disunity, Harmony and Discord: A Response to Lillegard and Davenport," in *Kierkegaard After MacIntyre: Essays on Freedom, Narrative, and Virtue*, ed. John J. Davenport and Anthony Rudd (Chicago IL: Open Court Publishing, 2001) 329.

[20] Rudd, "In Defence of Narrative," 65–66.

claim, as I have argued Kierkegaard does, that a fully adequate self-understanding requires a narrative construal, is not to suggest that any particular construal at a given time is beyond questioning and criticizing. A tale is told to an audience; and that means criticism and revision are always possibilities.

The problem of self-deception can be put in terms of a problem of selection. Lippitt writes, "In selecting the material for our life narratives, what *justifies* the selection?"[21] But Kierkegaard, for one, is well aware of the role of selection in a narrative self-understanding. As I argued in an earlier chapter, the controlled use of irony allows one to discern those aspects of one's actuality that do not relate to one's gift and task. Understanding the structure of the moral life in terms of gift and task, then, provides one with a principle for a non-arbitrary selection of material. Cast into a narrative form, the result will be not completely comprehensive, as if told from a divine point of view, but it will be true and adequate to one's real identity.

But, in any event, the critics of narrative leave the alternative unclear. If the temptation to self-deception is enough to cause us to lay aside narrative as the proper form of self-understanding, then what form will leave us unmoved by such temptations? Even Kant, not generally taken as a champion of narrative, noticed the possibilities for self-deception within his own framework. As John Hare notes, "On the one hand, Kant referred to 'man's self-conceit and the exaggeration of his powers'; on the other hand, 'we may [falsely] imagine that the moral law is indulgent as far as we are concerned.'"[22] In other words, to deal with the evident gap

---

[21] Lippitt, "Getting the Story Straight," 49.

[22] John E. Hare, *The Moral Gap: Kantian Ethics, Human Limits, and God's Assistance* (New York: Clarendon Press/Oxford University Press, 1996) 99.

between our moral capacity and the demands of the moral law, we may either, in Hare's terms, "puff up" our capacity or we may "reduce the demand." In either case, we deceive ourselves. It turns out, then, that the temptation to self-deception does not belong to narrative forms of self-understanding as such but rather to efforts to understand the self at all. Our task is not to find a form of self-interpretation that renders us impervious to self-deception but instead to engage in frequent, earnest, and accountable self-examination so that our illusions about ourselves can be dispelled.

Triviality. Some critics argue that, even if the claims of the narrativists are true, they are merely trivially true. John Christman, for example, avers that "what we are left with is that selves are individuals who reflect on experiences and events in a way that gives meaning to them."[23] Against the notion that humans typically understand themselves in narrative terms, Galen Strawson argues that "the claim is trivial," if it simply means that actions like making coffee require forethought and some kind of ordering.[24] Lamarque refers to the explanatory power of narratives as a "truism."[25]

The triviality objection is in one sense a concession. As Rudd notices, the critics seem to be granting that "the understanding of even simple human actions must take a narrative form," and he rightly maintains that this is "by no means a trivial point, given the continuing influence of rival,

---

Hare is citing Kant's *Lectures on Ethics*, trans. Louis Infield (Indianapolis IN: Hackett, 1930) 126; I have added the material in brackets for clarity.

[23] Christman, "Narrative Unity," 707.

[24] Strawson, "Against Narrativity," 439. Lippitt approvingly cites this passage; see Lippitt, "Getting the Story Straight," 37.

[25] Lamarque, "On Not Expecting Too Much from Narrative," 406.

scientistic models of action-explanation."[26] But any further response to it will require more clarity about the nature of the objection itself.

Critics who advance it seem to have three concerns in mind. First, they complain that the appeal to narrative fails to pick out morally significant action; if making coffee requires narrative display, then anything and everything does, rendering the very concept fairly uninteresting. Second, responding to claims that the ethical life has the unity of a narrative, they argue that the concept of narrative unity fails to pick out morally praiseworthy lives from among others. Finally, they suggest that the conditions for narrative are so minimal—consider Strawson's criteria of "forethought" and "order"—that the concept itself must be inconsequential.

The first objection assumes a view of the moral life that many advocates of narrative would refuse to concede. One might think, as the critics seem to do, that morally significant actions constitute a subset of human actions more generally, and one must sift through the latter to get to the former for purposes of moral reflection. Because the narrative form does not assist in that sifting, the critics leave it aside as inconsequential. But an advocate of narrative may argue instead that the sets of actions are coextensive: every human action is a moral action. From that perspective, the narrative form does not repay attention because it picks out the morally relevant actions from the indifferent ones like making coffee; rather, attention to narrative is important precisely because it applies to every action and reveals that agents are always moving in relation to the human good at which they finally

[26] Rudd, "In Defence of Narrative," 63. As if to underscore Rudd's contention, Christman frequently uses "events" where one might expect to see "actions," as in the quote above.

aim. This is most assuredly a controversial view, but there's no reason to think it trivial.[27]

The second form of this objection perhaps poses more difficulty. Lippitt develops it extensively in relation to the ethical critique of the aesthete, claiming that both the ethical life and aesthetic life are capable of narrative unity, so that this criterion cannot serve to differentiate the one from the other. Anyone, he argues, can tell an intelligible story about his life that suggests some rough-and-ready unity to it.

But in this argument, he ignores one of his own critical claims. Against his interpretation of Rudd and other defenders of narrative, Lippitt insists that Judge William does not offer a formal concept of narrative unity as leverage for cracking the aesthetic mask of despair. Instead, says Lippitt, Judge William relies on a number of substantive claims, including claims about God, providence, and so forth. I think Lippitt is right to demand that we read Judge William with an eye to his substantive claims as well as the formal aspects of his arguments. But if we apply that insight to the objection before us, then we will also turn to the substantive claims implicated in Kierkegaard's use of narrative before dismissing that use as trivial.

With Rudd and his allies, I think we might well say that a distinctive mark of the ethical life is its narrative unity; but we must also remember that, in Kierkegaard's view, that means the unity of a story beginning with a gift that is also a task. Every form of despair seeks to deny the gift or to develop it in

[27] Stokes makes use of just this point to argue that the self can be unified through the assumption of responsibility for each of its moments, surely a significant claim. But Stokes's explanation of the moral significance of eating cereal in terms of its possible implication in some structural injustice is too narrow; the virtue of temperance and its counterpart vice in gluttony, among other virtues and vices, provide a richer, more textured context. See Stokes, "Locke, Kierkegaard," 662–63.

a way that fails to correspond to its nature; the ethical life accepts the gift as gift and gratefully takes up the task of developing it in accord with its real integrity. Certainly a purely ethical approach will fail to comprehend the whole of that gift or the transfigured possibilities of its development in the light of faith. Nevertheless, a demarcation can be made here between the aesthetic on one side and the ethico-religious on the other. Thus, the appeal to narrative unity turns out not to be trivial but to be highly significant, though it may depend on controversial substantive claims about the structure of the moral life and even about the agency of divine providence. But Lippitt is right: wrestling with such substantive claims cannot be avoided if we are to come to terms with Kierkegaard's use of narrative.

The third form of the triviality objection argues that the conditions for narrative are so minimal as to render the concept inconsequential. Strawson, for example, refers to "forethought" and "order" as the basic conditions for narrative; other critics offer similarly minimal criteria. One might first note that whether such conditions render narrative trivial depends on precisely what they mean. Taking Strawson's conditions, for example, one might argue that forethought, if it means forethought of the human good towards which one strives, is quite interesting; and order, too, if it implies an ordering to or away from that good, would also prove worthy of attention. Reading forethought and order in the context of human life understood as gift and task would yield just such interpretations; these conditions turn out not so much to be minimal as crucial. If they yield narratives, as Strawson suggests, then one has every reason to expect those narratives to be of importance.

In any case, though, these minimal conditions fail to capture a view like Kierkegaard's implied account of narrative. As I argued above, Kierkegaard's understanding of human life in terms of its gift and task entails that reflection on it must take the form of a tale told by a teller expressing a point of view. This more robust sense of narrative is what is at stake in these debates, not the more desiccated version suggested by the critics. Thus the objection in this form attempts something like a bait-and-switch that finally fails to bring home its target.

Hubris and Over-Simplification. Perhaps the critics are most insistent in their accusation of hubris. They routinely charge the advocates of narrative with an overweening and distorting sense of self-importance, usually using terms of grandiosity. Lamarque insists that "the whole idea of a 'life-narrative' is far too literary and grandiose,"[28] arguing that the stories we tell about ourselves are "for the most part blandly true rather than grandly inventive."[29] Christman suggests that the different parts of a human life "fail to interconnect in a grand scheme."[30] Drawing on Christman's arguments, Lippitt denies that he feels "any obligation to bring each and every aspect of my life under one grand narrative."[31] Strawson accuses narrative theorists such as Charles Taylor and Paul Ricoeur of being "motivated by a sense of their own importance or significance that is absent in other human beings."[32] He goes on to suggest that this apparent hubris derives from their being "wrapped up in forms of religious belief,"[33] and quickly dismisses

---

[28] Lamarque, "On Not Expecting Too Much from Narrative," 405.
[29] Ibid., 403.
[30] Christman, "Narrative Unity as a Condition of Personhood," 704.
[31] Lippitt, "Getting the Story Straight," 46.
[32] Strawson, "Against Narrativity," 436.
[33] Ibid., 437.

religious belief itself as "one of the most fundamental vehicles of human narcissism."[34]

What could motivate these passionate denunciations of hubris in the narrativist camp? To get a sense of the deeper issues, one must first recognize that the critics are not objecting primarily to the usefulness of narrative for explaining or recounting human action in a piecemeal fashion. They deny instead that the unity of a narrative is an ethical ideal for a human life, or at least for all human lives. In Kierkegaard's terms, they reject the existence of a highest task grounding all others. Underlying this rejection is almost always a strong conviction that the goods of a human life are plural, incommensurable, and most likely in conflict. These critics seem to propose a dilemma: *either* one recognizes the plurality and likely conflict between human goods and so eschews efforts to shoehorn them into one pattern of value *or* one seeks to maximize one type of value, taking it, in John Rawls's phrase, as a "dominant end."[35]

If one opts for the second horn of the dilemma, then one must pretend to a kind of control over one's life and circumstances that is more god-like than human and at the same time suffer from a blindness to the real though conflicting values open to us. That first consequence leads to the charge of hubris; the second one leads to a related charge of over-simplification. Quinn expresses the latter criticism by describing "the pressure to simplify by exclusion that the yearning for unity and wholeness puts on ethical life."[36] In a world of incommensurable and conflicting values, one can achieve unity only by excluding those real goods that compete

[34] Ibid., 437n18.

[35] Rawls, *A Theory of Justice*, 552–53.

[36] Quinn, "Unity and Disunity," 330.

with the dominant end one has chosen to pursue. So, though parts of our lives may be rendered in narrative form, any attempt to understand our whole lives in the unity of a narrative will require a blinding hubris.

The previous chapter's reading of *Works of Love* provides the resources for responding to the second of these two related charges. I considered there a criticism of Kierkegaard's doctrine on love structurally parallel to the over-simplification charge. Kierkegaard, some say, replaces ordinary human loves with the rigor of neighbor love, thus reducing the moral life to something inhuman. I argued in response that attention to the implicit narratives in *Works of Love* shows that Kierkegaard does not replace ordinary human loves but contextualizes them. That text also makes clear that the relation of an agent to an ultimate good does not have to be maximizing, in the way critics sometimes assume. If my argument there is convincing, then it does not follow that a search for unity must result in a blindness to available human goods. It follows, too, that it is not hubristic to seek to shape one's life so that it all becomes intelligible within that context of commanded love.[37]

A critic might respond that my account does not make room for goods that so fundamentally conflict that they cannot be rendered intelligible from within the same context. But that response simply goes to show that the real challenge here is not to narrative unity but instead to a certain view of the

[37] Quinn does recognize that one might think of an infinite, uncreated good as a legitimate "total and exclusive focus of our aspirations." Then he suggests that the Christian interpretation of that possibility contains just the kind of conflict he has in mind, since love of God competes with love of neighbor and a "balance" of the two conflicting goods must be sought. But, of course, on my reading of *Works of Love,* love of God and love of neighbor cannot compete on the same level and so do not call for a coordination in terms of balancing equal but conflicting goods. See Quinn, "Unity and Disunity," 330.

human good. The charges of hubris and over-simplification reveal a fundamental difference; in Strawson's words, though in a slightly different context, they show that "we have here yet another deep divider of the human race."[38] Plato, Aristotle, St. Thomas Aquinas, and the bulk of the Western tradition have always maintained that there is some final good that provides an ultimate horizon of meaning for the many goods we pursue; but many, perhaps most, modern and contemporary philosophers have rejected that thesis, taking it as plainly evident that human goods are fundamentally in conflict in such a way that they escape any ultimate context that can contain them all.[39] This is a deep division; and though I would not say that it is beyond the reach of reasoned argument, an examination of the case for and against the significance of narrative in ethics is not the place to achieve a final resolution.

Kierkegaard on the Limits of Narrative

But something more can be said without straying too far from the narrative theme. Throughout his defense of narrative, Rudd emphasizes the role narratives play in rendering action intelligible. In the course of that argument, he writes, "But intelligibility is not an all or nothing matter; the wider the narrative, the more context that is given, the more intelligible the action becomes, though ultimate intelligibility is a limit concept, which could only be actual for God (or Hegel)." Here again we find the concept of an ultimate context, a final frame in which everything else comes into focus. Though not using

---

[38] Strawson, "Against Narrativity," 437.

[39] Some defenders of narrative belong in this latter group. John Davenport, for example, is emphatic about his allegiance to the more modern view; see his "Towards an Existential Virtue Ethics: Kierkegaard and MacIntyre," in *Kierkegaard After MacIntyre*, 291–94. See also Rudd, "In Defence of Narrative," 64–65.

the language of a *summum bonum*, Rudd does suggest here that all human goods find their intelligible place in a single context. He further specifies that context as narrative and as regulative. In other words, we have narrative all the way down; but that final narrative is, in fact, nothing more than a regulative ideal (at least for us).[40]

In this section, I argue that Kierkegaard's own view about the ultimate context for our particular narratives differs in significant ways from Rudd's. In particular, for Kierkegaard that context is not another narrative but a moment. The aesthetic moment, of course, must be contextualized in a narrative, as Rudd and others have rightly pointed out. But there is another kind of moment, an "atom of eternity" that is the "fullness of time," that marks an encounter with the divine and thus, in Kierkegaard's view, transcends and sustains the narratives of our lives. Such a moment, or analogues to it, can be found in the sacraments, in promises, in joy, and in the judgments of conscience. And it is in those places that we come up against the limits of narrative.

Narrative and the Moment in Either/Or. The first part of *Either/Or* consists of the papers of a fictional character who represents the aesthetic life-view, and includes a variety of texts by different characters and in different genres. "The Seducer's Diary" comprises the journals of a man named Johannes, who records his efforts to woo a young girl named Cordelia. His ruminations prompt him to describe a plan for a

---

[40] Rudd, "In Defence of Narrative," 64. Rudd perhaps has in mind here Climacus's claim that, though there cannot be a system of existence for us, there can be for God. But a system is an objective perspective; Climacus's point is that we cannot escape being participants in temporal striving, whereas God's eternity means that he does not play that role and so has a different perspective. We must not pretend to be God. Can "narrative" function in Rudd's argument in the same way that "system" does in Climacus's? I'm not so sure. See Kierkegaard, *Postscript*, 1:118-19.

book, to be titled, "A Contribution to a Theory of the Kiss."[41] As part of the theory, he considers various classification schemes for kisses. After discarding a scheme that turns on the sounds kisses make—"language does not have an adequate range for my observations," he decides—he turns to the category of time. And he finds in that category the most important classificatory principle: "The first kiss," he argues, "is qualitatively different from all others."[42] The first kiss thus exists in its own moment, at the beginning of a history between two lovers but also somehow transcending that history. The first kiss represents first love—not the first person one loved but rather the first moment you and your beloved realized you were in love.

For the aesthete, first love is the pinnacle of romance. First love, like the first kiss, exists in a moment qualitatively differentiated from others; but the next moment is only quantitatively differentiated from those that follow. Lovers turn from their first kiss to face simply one moment after another in a long and monotonous series. So Johannes says of his engagement to Cordelia, "I take the girl, she takes me—and now the story begins."[43] And two paragraphs later, he announces, "What I must do now is...prepare everything for the breaking-off of the engagement, so as to ensure a more beautiful and more significant relationship with Cordelia."[44] After having the satisfaction of bringing Cordelia to the moment of first love and then breaking off the engagement to preserve its qualitatively unique purity, the last paragraphs of Johannes's diary find him planning a new conquest, looking

---

[41] Kierkegaard, *Either/Or*, 1:416.
[42] Ibid., 1:417.
[43] Ibid., 1:312.
[44] Ibid., 1:313.

forward to a new variation that can provoke again the moment of first love.

In the second volume of *Either/Or,* Judge William, representing an ethical life-view, responds to "The Seducer's Diary" and the other papers of the first volume by attempting to illuminate the self-defeating nature of aesthetic love. He argues that first love contains within itself a desire to last beyond the moment; after all, no lover has ever whispered across a candle-lit table, "I am yours—for the next 10 days." But as long as the aesthete identifies love with the qualitatively distinct moment, that natural aspiration must go unfulfilled, since the ecstatic moment must inevitably pass. Marital love, however, is love in history, and so it incorporates the passing of moments into its nature; hence, it can fulfill first love's longing for permanence.

Consequently, Judge William urges his reader to eschew the search for the ecstatic moment. Against the aesthete's valorizing of the qualitatively differentiated moment of first love, Judge William champions the narrative structure of marriage, in which significance is found in the succession of ordinary moments, moments only quantitatively distinct from each other.

To clarify his claim, Judge William distinguishes between outer and inner history, considering how each might be artistically represented. An outer history is a story of how one conquers external obstacles or attains an external goal, like a fairy-tale prince battling dragons and searching for the princess he loves. The interest in these stories lies in the moments of conflict and victory; in artistic representation, they can be foreshortened or concentrated on the key moments that give point to the others. An inner history, on the other hand, is a story of how one overcomes the temptations to despair and distraction coming from the pressures of time itself. The struggle, then, is to remain constant in the succession of moments, and so each little moment counts as much as the others. Judge William argues that, though an inner history has genuine beauty, it cannot be represented artistically, as can an outer history, since any representation would require foreshortening. He provides a series of contrasts to fill out this point:

> Romantic love can be portrayed very well in the moment; marital love cannot, for an ideal husband is not one who is ideal once in his life but one who is that every day. If I wish to portray a hero who conquers kingdoms and countries, this can be done very well in the moment, but a cross-bearer who takes up his cross every day can never be portrayed in either poetry or art, for the point is that he does it every day. ...Courage can be concentrated very well in the moment; patience cannot, precisely because patience contends against time.[45]

If the beauty of marriage, discipleship, and patience cannot be portrayed in art, then how can it be represented? Judge William answers: "by being lived." The beauty of first love is not available for the married; but their lives themselves have become objects of beauty. So not only is it the case that the aesthete's project is self-defeating; it is also true that marital love makes beauty an even more integral and lasting part of its nature than the aesthetic can.

The arguments of the aesthete and the judge anticipate, to some degree, the contemporary debate about narrative. In that perspective, the aesthete emerges as the champion of Strawson's "Episodics" and their allies, struggling for the beauty and value of those moments, like that of first love, that cannot be subsumed under some grand, overarching narrative.

---

[45] Ibid., 2:135.

The aesthete, open to the moment that does not fit into a pre-determined narrative, orients himself to the "adventure" that the critics of narrativists accuse them of missing.[46] But the judge sees the aesthete as "fighting for the moment against time," a fight that must be futile because its prize is that which "has disappeared."[47] Stressing the values of unity and continuity, Judge William insists that only the inner history of marriage can truly manifest and preserve the aesthetic values of the moment, marking him, it would seem, as the prototype of today's defenders of narrative.

Just as they do, the judge focuses on the virtues displayed through a temporal sequence. The inner history of a marriage is a story of virtues such as patience, faithfulness, constancy, humility, perseverance, and so on.[48] These virtues belong together because they are all excellences of our struggle with time. They are evident in time taken extensively across a complete sequence of ordinary moments, not intensively in a qualitatively distinct moment.[49] As Climacus would say, they represent tasks that last as long as one's life. Understanding one's life in terms of the aesthetic moment, then, can only mislead one, as defenders of narrative are quick to point out.

But there the similarity ends, because the judge explicitly denies that the inner history of a marriage, that is, of a life lived ethically, can be represented in any way, even as a story. In this way, he anticipates not the defenders of narrative but the critics who insist that the literary narratives favored by the defenders cannot be pressed into service as forms of representing and understanding an actual human life. As it turns out, for Judge William, one cannot understand one's life

---

[46] See, for example, Lippitt, "Getting the Story Straight," 52, 57–58.

[47] Kierkegaard, *Either/Or*, 2:141.

[48] Ibid., 2:139.

[49] Ibid., 2:138.

in terms of a narrative any more than one can in terms of ecstatic and isolated moments. In Scholes's and Kellogg's terms, a narrative requires a tale and a teller; in Judge William's vocabulary, a narrative is a representation of a sequence of moments. To tell the inner history of a task that takes a lifetime would require a lifetime, unless the teller selects only those moments that serve the climax of the story. Judge William calls this process of selection "foreshortening" and understands that it is essential for poetic and artistic representations. But the inner histories of the virtues the judge recommends cannot be foreshortened, for doing so would require that some moment stand out qualitatively as a criterion for the selection of others. And the point to these virtues is that they are not manifested in an ecstatic moment but precisely in the succession of ordinary moments.

In other words, the inner histories that Judge Williams poses against the aesthete's abstracted moments are, paradoxically, stories that cannot be told. Telling them would require selecting some moments rather than others. But such a process would require constituting some particular moment as a criterion, in which case the story one tells would end up being an outer rather than an inner history. Thus, artistic or poetic productions—literary narratives—fail as forms for the understanding of human life lived ethically. Such a life cannot be understood but only lived.

To be sure, the judge insists that its living will have a dramatic structure. The summit of the ethical life, which brings "into actual existence the highest in aesthetics," is only achieved by him "who feels himself present as a character in a drama the deity is writing," and not only present as a character but fully adopting the role assigned.[50] This dramatic vision of

---

[50] Ibid., 2:137.

the best life is surely a far cry from the romantic irony championed by the aesthete. But it is not a form of self-understanding; it describes not the backward glance by which we understand our lives and their course to our present place, but the forward look in which we adopt a course to follow for the future. In fact, Judge William more often alludes to music than to narrative or drama as an analogy for the ethical life. After insisting that the aesthetic can only be represented by being lived, he comments, "It thereby has a similarity to music, which is only because it is continually repeated, is only in the moment of being performed."[51] A song, on the judge's view, cannot be without being performed; being a song and representing a song, therefore, cannot be separated. And further, it would seem, one cannot understand a song apart from its performance. Likewise, the ethical life cannot be without being lived, and so cannot be understood in any representation other than the living of that life itself.

Granted, in the judge's analogy, the actor "feels that he himself wants to say what is being whispered to him" by the poet/prompter, but that vague feeling can hardly count as a deep or sophisticated self-understanding. Perhaps here we have found the source of some criticisms commonly directed at the judge by those who find him too self-satisfied, too crude in his self-understanding. The last part of *Either/Or*, for example, is a sermon sent by the judge to the aesthete, and many readers take it as a critique of the judge as much as of his friend. Yet the judge seems not to recognize the sermon's critical edge. Or again, the judge's insistence that his life is a sacrifice for his family, and then his denial and rephrasing of that description into "finding joy," suggests an unconscious but quite real irony and dissatisfaction underlying the judge's glowing reports

---

[51] Ibid.

about his own life. Perhaps these blind spots result from Judge William's inability to take up a reflective stance on his life as a whole because he is convinced that such a perspective must smuggle in the aesthete's false transcendence in the qualitatively intensive moment. Taken all together, then, the judge's arguments suggest crucial flaws in both the aesthete's resistance to narrative and in his own attempts to present an alternative grounded in an inner history. The judge leaves his reader wondering whether self-understanding is finally possible at all or whether both the defenders of narrative and their critics represent dead ends in morally responsible self-reflection.

The Fullness of Time. Any attempt at a Kierkegaardian answer to those questions must bear in mind that Judge William's is not the last word in Kierkegaard's authorship, and later pseudonymous texts suggest a necessary contextualizing of the aesthete's and the judge's claims about moments and narratives. For Johannes, remember, the story of his attempts to seduce Cordelia matter only because they are the prerequisites for the ecstatic moment of first love. Judge William turns this relation inside out by describing inner history in such a way that the narrative takes priority over the moment, but then seems to succumb to some form of the moral blindness feared by critics of narrative.

Judge William is surely right to critique the illusory and self-defeating transcendence of the abstracted moment. But one must not neglect the possibility that there may be more than one kind of moment, more than one kind of transcendence. Some of Kierkegaard's other pseudonyms suggest that that possibility should be taken more seriously, giving us reasons to look for moments that can transcend and thus contextualize narrative self-understanding without reducing to the abstracted moment of the aesthetic imagination. In this section, I will adduce from those pseudonyms some comments that may evoke a more helpful concept of a transcendent moment and then provide some examples of such a moment by briefly considering sacraments, promises, joy, and conscience.

In *The Concept of Anxiety*, Vigilius Haufniensis discusses the concept of the moment in relation to time and eternity as part of his attempt to explain the transition to sin. Time, he says, is that which "'passes by.'" So, in relation to time, the moment is that empty abstraction that we imagine as the space between the past as it passes out of view and the future as it comes into view. Eternity, on the other hand, is not empty abstraction but "the infinitely contentful present,"[52] the fullness that gives significance to the passing moments of time. In relation to eternity, then, the moment is not empty abstraction but the touching of time by eternity.[53] Johannes Climacus, another pseudonym, puts it this way: "A moment such as this is unique. To be sure, it is short and temporal, as the moment is; it is passing, as the moment is, past, as the moment is in the next moment, and yet it is decisive, and yet it is filled with the eternal. A moment such as this must have a special name. Let us call it: *the fullness of time*."[54] Haufniensis calls the same kind of moment "an atom of eternity," as opposed to an "atom of time." The senses of transcendence these two concepts of the moment represent diverge just as they do. The transcendence of an atom of time is the one sought by the aesthete, a transcendence liberated from the bonds of continuity that comprise the narrative. But the atom of eternity transcends the temporal succession not by abandoning it but by gathering it

---

[52] Kierkegaard, *Concept of Anxiety*, 86–87.

[53] Ibid., 89.

[54] Kierkegaard, *Philosophical Fragments*, 18.

up in such a way that one is returned to it with a deeper sense of its significance. The moment as atom of eternity is thus the condition for a narrative of repetition of the higher kind. So it is qualitatively and not just quantitatively distinct from the other moments in a narrative; and yet it also has its place in a quantitative succession. It is a moment, but a moment that abides.[55]

The insights belonging here to Haufniensis and Climacus do not require one to discard the incisive critique of the aesthetic that Judge William provides. Rather, one might expect the two later pseudonyms to agree with the judge that the aesthetic moment must be contextualized in a narrative if it is to avoid defeating its own ambitions. And yet they encourage the reader to consider that the contextualizing narrative needs its own justification; like the moment, it cannot sustain its own significance. And any attempt to make the narrative self-justifying will prove just as self-defeating as the illusory transcendence of the aesthetic moment. To put it in terms of Judge William's concerns: just as romantic rapture cannot sustain its momentary significance without the wider context of the story of a marriage, so a marital narrative cannot sustain its significance without some more determinative context. And that more determinative context, Haufniensis's and Climacus's observations suggest, is the moment, now rendered as an atom of eternity, a moment that abides because it has within in it the fullness of time, because it gathers within itself the sense of the narrative as a whole.

---

[55] James Collins eloquently summarizes this feature of Kierkegaard's thought and alludes to its connection to repetition when he writes, "Transcendence does not lead away from actuality in its human mode but gives new meaning to what is concrete, temporal, and contingent...by confessing the presence of the eternal being in the fullness of time, the *pleroma*." See *The Mind of Kierkegaard* (Princeton NJ: Princeton University Press, 1953; rep. 1983) 165.

In fact, in the *Philosophical Fragments* Climacus takes aim at a view much like the self-justifying narrative the judge suggests. In that text, Climacus contrasts the relation of learner and teacher from Socratic and Christian perspectives. Learning on a Socratic model is a process of recollection, drawing out from within oneself what is already there, though perhaps covered over by forgetfulness. On a Christian model, by contrast, learning essential truths is a matter of encounter, of coming to a Teacher—the God-Man—from whom one must receive both the truth as a gift and the condition for receiving the truth as a gift. Given this contrast, insisting on a Socratic picture of one's learning is to engage in idolatry, since it means replacing the divine teacher with oneself as the source of truth.

Judge William runs the risk of just this kind of idolatry, given his own immanentist critique of transcendence, for on his account, the essential truth of marriage is not something the married must receive from outside the story of their own efforts but rather something immanent within the narrative that brings their quotidian moments into coherence.[56] Consequently, the married are free to find in their own narratives the essential truth that reveals the meaning and significance of their marriage; and so the Teacher is not needed or not needed essentially for learning the truth of the marriage, though he may still be useful as a pointer to or reminder of the truth one already knows deep within. A thorough-going denial of transcendence quickly becomes an idolatry of the immanent.

To put the point in still broader terms, the collapse of the modern attempt to transcend the bounds of particularity and

---

[56] I grant that Judge William situates his defense of marriage in a theological context; yet I cannot put aside the suspicion that his theology is finally more pantheist than Christian. For Judge William, the married have eternity *in time*; the eternal just is the complete succession of their marital moments.

finitude in the abstracted moments occupied by thinking things, transcendental egos, and ideal spectators has led to an equally modern fixation with immanence, language games, and tournaments of narratives. The pendulum may swing from one extreme to the other, but the clock keeps the same time. And for both transcendent romanticism and immanent idolatry, the time never comes for humbly learning from the Teacher what cannot be excavated from within.

Sacraments and Promises. How can Haufniensis and Climacus help us to see a way out? The atom of eternity Haufniensis describes captures Climacus's moment of learning from the Teacher, a moment that is transcendent without being illusory. If we are attentive, we can see this dynamic working in more than one way in our own experience. From a Christian perspective, we have first the sacraments. Communion on Fridays was an important event for Kierkegaard, and, from a different angle of tradition, the *Catechism of the Catholic Church* describes Christ's paschal mystery, the source of the sacraments, in terms reminiscent of Haufniensis's "atom of eternity."

> His paschal mystery is a real event that occurred in our history, but it is unique; all other historical events happen once, and then they pass away, swallowed up in the past. The Paschal mystery of Christ, by contrast, cannot remain only in the past, because by his death he destroyed death, and all that Christ is—all that he did and suffered for all men—participates in the divine eternity, and so transcends all times while being made present in them all. The event of the Cross and Resurrection *abides* and draws everything toward life.[57]

The Paschal mystery, like the sacraments that make it present, was a moment in a quantitative succession, a moment

[57] *Catechism of the Catholic Church* (Allen TX: Thomas More, 1994) §1085.

that passed by like all temporal moments. And yet it is a qualitatively distinct moment because it transcends the succession of moments and gives that continuous temporal movement its point and purpose, "draw[ing] everything toward life." The mystery of Christ thus transcends the narratives by which the succession of our temporal moments achieve their unity, and yet it does not do so by romantic abstraction from that succession. Because it transcends our own stories, it can endow them with meaning; because it is a moment within those stories, its transcendence is not self-defeating and the meaning it grants is not illusory.[58]

To bring this dynamic nearer to Judge William's interest in love and marriage, consider a second way it makes a constant appearance in our lives, namely, the phenomenon of the promise. As Judge William insists, marriage itself is constituted by a mutual promise, the exchange of vows between bride and groom. That moment of promise, though simply one among the moments of their lives together, stands out qualitatively because of the nature of such promises. Guy Mansini's observations about "life promises" are apposite:

> The transcendence of time—from within time—that such promises bespeak reveals the whole complexity of man, metaphysical and moral. Metaphysically, this transcendence of time is spirit, but as exercised only from within time, it is also bodily. Morally, a choice, a decision that in such promising intends the whole can itself be but a sketch, an outline. It is not

---

[58] Note that Collins plausibly argues that, though Kierkegaard's understanding of the Incarnation recognized its nature as a moment that abides, his insistence on its utter uniqueness prevented him from fully recognizing its status as a source of later historical events, like those of the sacramental life of the Church: "The contemporaneity of each individual believer with Christ tends to cancel out the ordinary historical process and abandon to meaningless triviality the secular generations and their travail" (Collins, *Mind of Kierkegaard*, 173).

> immediate possession of the intended, but a mere stretching toward it. It is more empty than full, and the filling requires many trips to the well.[59]

The moment of the promise transcends the succession of moments that follows it only because in the promise that future is gathered up and made a gift to the other. By means of a promise, I can give my future to another, surrendering my right to consider my future as at my disposal without regard for the other. The moment of promising is thus always qualitatively distinct from the narrative that follows, even if that moment is also always one among others and requires the others finally to determine its content. Marital vows, then, transcend the quotidian routines of the household because it was by means of those vows that today's household moments were first and definitively given to the other; and yet the vows cannot float free of the everyday because those routine episodes give to the promise a content that one could not have imagined when first making it. Since a promise without a story is intelligible only as a tragedy or a defeat, the narrative retains its own significance in relation to the transcendence of a promise; and yet, at the same time, the promise serves as a reminder that the meaning of the story cannot be dredged out from within, as if it were self-justifying.

Joy. In *The Lily of the Field and the Birds of the Air*, Kierkegaard gives us another picture of this dynamic. The third of the three devotional discourses in this small collection concerns joy, which Kierkegaard describes as being "present to oneself...*today*"; or, in other words, "Joy is the present time with the whole emphasis on: *the present time*."[60] It might seem

[59] Guy Mansini, OSB, *Promising and the Good* (Naples FL: Sapientia Press, 2005) 54.

[60] Søren Kierkegaard, *Without Authority*, ed. and trans. Howard V. Hong and Edna H. Hong (Princeton NJ: Princeton University Press, 1997) 39.

that the joyful one must not understand himself narratively, since his focus on the present moment shifts attention away from the past and the future. In fact, this third discourse taken by itself might suggest an additional objection to narrative self-understanding: by focusing on the past and future as a horizon for one's present, one becomes distracted precisely from that whole-hearted attention to the present moment that undergirds joy and appears as a virtue to many who think carefully about a morally and spiritually well-lived life.[61]

But a closer look reveals that the discourse conditions the joy of being present to oneself *today* on the themes of the previous two discourses, silence and obedience. One who has developed the virtue of silence waits on God, listens to him, and believes him. One who is silent becomes aware that he is before God,[62] excluding from his awareness every "third factor."[63] For the silent one, God is "the one and only," not merely one among many.[64] Silence thus leads to obedience,[65] because the silent one knows that God demands unconditional obedience, just as a lover demands unconditional devotion.[66]

But obedience itself assumes an acknowledgement of providence, a trust that begins in silence. Kierkegaard writes that the silent one knows that "everything takes place in its time," that "spring will come in due season."[67] Thus silence acknowledges a divine plan directing all things to come to

---

[61] For a recent example, see Pierre Hadot, "Only the Present is our Happiness: The Value of the Present Instant in Goethe and in Ancient Philosophy," in *Philosophy as a Way of Life: Spiritual Exercises from Socrates to Foucault*, ed. Arnold I. Davidson and trans. Michael Chase (Malden, MA: Blackwell, 1995) 217-237.

[62] Kierkegaard, *Without Authority*, 17.

[63] Ibid., 22.

[64] Ibid., 23.

[65] Ibid., 25.

[66] Ibid., 23–24.

[67] Ibid., 13.

fruition in their proper time and season. This theme continues in the discussion of obedience. The obedient *"believe that everything that happens is unconditionally God's will."*[68] Furthermore, God's will is directed to the flourishing of the potential that he gives to his creatures. By obedience, says Kierkegaard, "one became itself in beauty."[69] But in refusing to obey, a human being "would not fulfill his potentiality, which nevertheless was granted to him."[70]

Of course, one remembers this language of gift, potentiality, and becoming what one is from the discussion of providence in the *Concept of Irony*, where it suggests a narrative form;[71] so here one should note that joy, presence to oneself in the present moment, is conditioned on virtues that recognize one's place in a larger narrative, though not one of one's own devising. Precisely because the narrative context is that of divine providence, the individual can rest joyfully in the present moment without losing himself in rushing forward to create a new future or loitering in a past he is loath to surrender. The presence to oneself *today* that originally appeared as a challenge to a narrative self-understanding is finally revealed as conditioned on a particular kind of narrative self-reflection.

Kierkegaard also formulates this insight in another way, coming closer to the vocabulary of Haufniensis and Clim-acus. In the first discourse, he writes, "only by being silent does one find the moment. ...[T]he moment *is* only in silence."[72] Likewise, he insists in the second discourse that "only unconditional obedience can with unconditional accuracy find

---

[68] Ibid., 26. Emphasis original.
[69] Ibid., 28.
[70] Ibid.
[71] See the discussion in ch. 1.
[72] Kierkegaard, *Without Authority*, 14.

the moment." He does not contradict himself here, because true silence and obedience are mutually implicating. He does, however, find a way to emphasize the importance of the moment in the kind of virtuous life he is expounding. One who has cultivated silence, obedience, and joy finds himself in the present moment because it is a moment in the narrative of divine providence. But it is not only a moment in a narrative; it is at the same time a moment that transcends the narrative. Kierkegaard writes of those who failed to grow in these virtues "that they were never aware of the moment, that in their lives the eternal and the temporal are exclusively separated."[73] The moment that silence and obedience find, the moment that joy takes pleasure in, is a moment in which the eternal becomes manifest. The silent and obedient are "unconditionally undisturbed by the next moment,"[74] because they know that that moment, too, contains the eternal. The moment in which they find themselves is, thus, the "atom of eternity," the "moment that abides," because in it they find themselves before the eternal and changeless God, who remains the same at each moment in the narrative he is writing. Without the eternal, the narrative itself cannot become the occasion of joy; but a moment in which one can find oneself before the eternal, though it is but a passing moment, can endow the whole narrative with an eternal significance.[75]

---

[73] Ibid.

[74] Ibid., 29.

[75] It is instructive to compare these discourses to treatments of the abandonment to divine providence frequently recommended by spiritual writers. Reginald Garrigou-Lagrange, OP, in Part IV of his *Providence*, [trans. Dom Bede Rose, OSB (St. Louis MO: B. Herder Book Co., 1937; Rep., Rockford, IL: TAN Books and Publishers, 1998)], surveys some of this literature, and his discussion reveals the same dynamic: to find the duty and the grace of the present moment, one must see it against the backdrop of divine providence; and, in turn, the apprehension of providence in the present moment grants the whole of one's history a deep significance. Garrigou-Lagrange cites such

Conscience. In *An Occasional Discourse,* also known as *Purity of Heart Is to Will One Thing,* Kierkegaard repeats this dynamic, describing the voice of conscience as that moment that transcends the narrative of one's life while at the same time endowing it with meaning. I will argue for this reading of the discourse in the present section. But, to set the stage by way of contrast, I will begin with some comments by John Lippitt, who appeals to this text as evidence that Kierkegaard has no special place for the significance of narratives. He notes that the discourse focuses on unity of the self. But he continues, "Such unity is not 'narrative unity,' insofar as narrative unity focuses upon our nature as *temporal* beings." Lippitt claims that the discourse "downgrades the temporal in relation to the eternal," because "the essential unity valorized by *Purity of Heart* is not narrative unity" but an eternal unity.[76] If Lippitt's reading is correct, then in this discourse Kierkegaard is arguing that self-interpretation must *not* take a narrative form, just because narratives fail to display the true unity that belongs essentially only to the eternal.

However, we have good reason to think Lippitt has missed the mark in his interpretation of the discourse. One might first note, as a general point, that Lippitt assumes attributing essential unity to the eternal means to deny it to the temporal. But, in fact, as I argued in another connection in chapter 4, the temporal and the eternal are not competitors.

---

authors as St. Francis de Sales, Bossuet, and de Caussade and summarizes their views this way: "We should not be satisfied with viewing the present moment along the horizontal line of time, as the connecting link between a vanished past and an uncertain temporal future; we ought rather to view it along that vertical line of time which links it up with the unique instant of unchanging eternity" (251). See also 241 where he relies on the constant relationship between each moment and our last end (Kierkegaard's "highest task") to make a similar point.

[76] Lippitt, "Getting the Story Straight," 51.

That unity belongs essentially to the eternal does not at all imply that unity does not belong in any sense to the temporal. Or, to put it in other words, the unity of the temporal does not have to be the same as that of the eternal to constitute, in its way, a true unity.

A look at some detail in the text makes the point even clearer. The discourse is divided into four sections: a first, unnumbered section setting the stage for the whole work by speaking of sin and confession; a second and third section (numbered one and two) describing purity of heart and the vice of double-mindedness; and a final section (numbered three) returning more directly to the occasion at hand and preparing the reader for the "holy act"[77] of confession. Conscience plays an important role in the framing sections, and Kierkegaard begins by relating conscience to the narrative of a human life.

The first section begins with a number of temporal images and a meditation on the Solomonic insight that "everything has its time."[78] After tracing a series of changes through a human life, ending with old age, Kierkegaard asks, "But is the story finished here?"[79] He concludes that there is more to a human life than the succession of moments by comparing stories of humans and of animals. They are both much the same in comprising a series of moments, in which the appropriate activity changes with the moment, and ending in old age and death.[80] But immortality distinguishes the human from the animal; and immortality is not just a post-mortem reality but "would have to have been present every moment of its life."[81]

---

[77] Kierkegaard, *Upbuilding Discourses*, 19.

[78] Ibid., 8.

[79] Ibid., 9.

[80] Ibid., 10.

[81] Ibid.

To be immortal is to have a larger context in which the temporal sequence plays out. As Kierkegaard puts it, "Immortality could not be a final change that intervened, if one wants to put it that way, in death as the concluding age; on the contrary it is a changelessness that is not changed with the change of years."[82] To possess immortality is not just to look forward to a quantitative addition to one's life but to possess now a qualitative difference.

Immortality cannot be reduced to the temporal sequence, or it would not distinguish the human from the animal story. But neither is it alien to that series of moments. Kierkegaard writes, "If, then, there is something eternal in a human being, this must be able to be and able to be claimed throughout every change."[83] The eternal in a human being is not alien to his temporal changes but rather exists in each successive change and can be appropriated in each time. Everything has its time; the time for dancing, for example, is now and then passes to make way for the time for mourning. But there is something, Kierkegaard insists, that always has its time in each change. And he names it as repentance and regret.[84] Repentance and regret are the voices of two guides, sent by providence, who "[watches] over every human being's journey through life."[85] "One calls forward to the good," explains Kierkegaard, "the other calls back from the evil."[86] The concluding section of the discourse suggests that these voices are the voice of conscience. Kierkegaard writes there, "eternity takes hold of each one separately with the strong arms of conscience."[87] The

[82] Ibid., 11.
[83] Ibid.
[84] Ibid., 13.
[85] Ibid.
[86] Ibid., 14.
[87] Ibid., 133.

judgments of conscience are, of course, passing moments in the temporal sequence that constitutes a human life; but, at the same time, they are something more. Their share in the changeless eternity of the good means that they are not simply passing moments but, from another angle, a moment that abides and pervades the temporal sequence.

An Occasional Discourse, then, does not reject the narrative unity of a human life for something else. Instead, we find in the discourse the same pattern we have found all along. Human life has a narrative form; but its unity and significance require not only the temporal sequence but also the context of a moment that transcends it and pervades it at the same time. Contrary to Lippitt's reading, the unity of a human life does not consist in becoming changelessly eternal but in the shaping of one's passing moments by right relation to the eternal. To reduce a human life to the narrative alone, shorn of the moment of encounter with a changeless eternity, would be to reduce it to the story of an animal. Yet to deny the narrative form of a human life would be a temptation to a despair of infinitude, a denial of the very substance to be transfigured by the transcendent moment. Kierkegaard leaves us, then, with a deep insight. We can fail to understand ourselves as moral agents because we try to see our lives in terms of scattered moments of ecstatic rupture or because we try to read them as nothing more than a self-consistent narrative. True self-understanding requires a confrontation with the eternal that, changeless, transcends our lives and yet pervades each moment.

Conclusion

I began this chapter with lines from Eliot that suggested the contextualizing of the isolated moment in the narrative pattern of the everyday. But Eliot did not leave things there any more than did Kierkegaard and his pseudonyms. Towards the end of "The Dry Salvages," he writes,

> ...to apprehend
> The point of intersection of the timeless
> with time, is an occupation for the saint—
> No occupation either, but something given
> And taken, in a lifetime's death in love,
> Ardour and selflessness and self-surrender.[88]

This point of intersection—"the still point of the turning world," as he puts it elsewhere[89]—is that point of transcendence in which the scattered moments of our lives are gathered up, receiving their significance as a gift from the only one who is Eternal. But the reception of that kind of transcendence requires a lifetime of ordinary moments in which we put the self to death in love; what the Eternal means when it touches time in a moment of pure gift can only be told by a story. And that's why Eliot ends with "the hint half guessed, the gift half understood, [which] is [the] Incarnation":[90] that is to say, with the moment that is, according to Climacus, the fullness of time, offering as gift the redemption of our everyday lives in our own narratives of repetition.

---

[88] Eliot, "Dry Salvages," *Four Quartets*, ll. 200–205.

[89] Eliot, "Burnt Norton," *Four Quartets*, l. 62.

[90] Eliot, "Dry Salvages," *Four Quartets*, l. 215. Bracketed material added for clarity.

Bibliography

Aristotle. *Nicomachean Ethics*. Translated by Terence Irwin. Indianapolis IN: Hackett Publishing Company, 1985.

———. *Poetics*. Translated by Ingram Bywater. In *The Basic Works of Aristotle*, edited by Richard McKeon. New York: Random House, 1941.

Barret, Lee. "The Neighbor's Material and Social Well-Being in Kierkegaard's *Works of Love*: Does It Matter?" In *International Kierkegaard Commentary: Works of Love*, edited by Robert L. Perkins, 137–65. Macon GA: Mercer University Press, 1999.

Battersby, James. "Narrativity, Self, and Self-Representation." *Narrative* 14 (January 2006): 27–44.

Berry, Wanda Warren. "Finally Forgiveness: Kierkegaard as a 'Springboard' for a Feminist Theology of Reform." In *Foundations of Kierkegaard's Vision of Community: Religion, Ethics, and Politics in Kierkegaard*, edited by George B. Connell and C. Stephen Evans, 196–217. Atlantic Highlands NJ: Humanities Press, 1992.

Booth, Wayne C. *The Company We Keep: An Ethics of Fiction*. Berkeley CA: University of California Press, 1988.

Burgess, Andrew J. "Patience and Expectancy in Kierkegaard's Upbuilding Discourses." In *Kierkegaard Studies: Yearbook*, edited by Niels Jørgen Cappelørn, Hermann Dueser, and Jon Stewart, 205–22. Berlin/New York: Walter de Gruyter, 2000.

Carroll, Noel. *Art in Three Dimensions*. New York: Oxford University Press, 2010.

———. "Narrative and the Ethical Life." In *Art and Ethical Criticism*, edited by Gary L. Hagberg, 35–62. Malden MA: Wiley-Blackwell, 2011.

Catechism of the Catholic Church. Allen TX: Thomas More, 1994.

Christman, John. "Narrative Unity as a Condition of Personhood." *Metaphilosophy* 35 (2004): 696–713.

Collins, James. *The Mind of Kierkegaard*. Princeton NJ: Princeton University Press, 1953; reprint 1983.

Crites, Stephen. "'The Blissful Security of the Moment': Recollection, Repetition, and Eternal
Recurrence." In *International Kierkegaard Commentary: Fear and Trembling and Repetition*, edited by Robert L. Perkins, 225–46. Macon GA: Mercer University Press, 1993.

Davenport, John J. "Towards an Existential Virtue Ethics: Kierkegaard and MacIntyre." In
Kierkegaard After MacIntyre: Essays on Freedom, Narrative, and Virtue, edited by John J. Davenport and Anthony Rudd, 265–323. Chicago IL: Open Court, 2001.

Dunning, Stephen. "Who Sets the Task: Kierkegaard on Authority." In *Foundations of Kierkegaard's Vision of Community*, edited by George B. Connell and C. Stephen Evans, 18–32. Atlantic Highlands NJ: Humanities Press, 1992.

Edwards, Jonathan. *The Nature of True Virtue*. Ann Arbor MI: University of Michigan Press, 1960.

Eliot, T. S. *Four Quartets*. New York: Harcourt Brace & Co., 1943.

Evans, C. Stephen. "Authority and Transcendence in *Works of Love*." In *Kierkegaard Studies Yearbook 1998*, edited by Niels Jorgen Cappelorn and Hermann Deuser with C. Stephen Evans, Alastair Hannay, and Bruce H. Kirmmse, 23–40. New York: Walter de Gruyter, 1998.

Ferreira, M. J. "Equality, Impartiality, and Moral Blindness in Kierkegaard's *Works of Love*."
Journal of Religious Ethics 25/1 (Spring 1997): 65–85.

———. *Love's Grateful Striving: A Commentary on Kierkegaard's* Works of Love. New York: Oxford University Press, 2001.

———. "Mutual Responsiveness in Relation: The Challenge of the Ninth Deliberation." In *International Kierkegaard Commentary: Works of Love*, edited by Robert L. Perkins, 193–209. Macon GA: Mercer University Press, 1999.

Garrigou-Lagrange, Reginald. *Providence*. Translated by Dom Bede Rose, OSB. St. Louis MO: B. Herder Book Co., 1937. Reprint, Rockford IL: TAN Books and Publishers, 1998.

Hadot, Pierre. "'Only the Present is our Happiness': The Value of the Present Instant in Goethe and in Ancient Philosophy." In *Philosophy as a Way of Life: Spiritual Exercises from Socrates to Foucault*, edited by Arnold I. Davidson. Translated by Michael Chase, 217-37. Malden MA: Blackwell Publishing, Ltd., 1995.

Grøn, Arne. "Temporality in Kierkegaard's Edifying Discourses." In *Kierkegaard Studies: Yearbook*, edited by Niels Jørgen Cappelørn, Hermann Dueser, and Jon Stewart, 191–204. New York: Walter de Gruyter, 2000.

Hannay, Alastair. *Kierkegaard: The Arguments of the Philosophers*. London: Routledge, 1991.

Hare, John E. *The Moral Gap: Kantian Ethics, Human Limits, and God's Assistance*. New York: Clarendon Press/Oxford University Press, 1996.

Jackson, Timothy P. "Arminian Edification: Kierkegaard on Grace and Free Will." In *The Cambridge Companion to Kierkegaard*, edited by Alastair Hannay and Gordon D. Marino, 235–56. Cambridge: Cambridge University Press, 1998.

Kant, Immanuel. *Lectures on Ethics*. Translated by Louis Infield. Indianapolis IN: Hackett, 1930.

Keeley, Louise Carroll. "Loving 'No One,' Loving Everyone: The Work of Love in Recollecting One Dead in Kierkegaard's *Works of Love*." In *International Kierkegaard Commentary: Works of Love*, edited by Robert L. Perkins, 211–48. Macon GA: Mercer University Press, 1999.

———. "Subjectivity and World in *Works of Love*." In *Foundations of Kierkegaard's Vision of Community*, edited by George B. Connell and C. Stephen Evans, 96–108. Atlantic Highlands NJ: Humanities Press, 1992.

Kierkegaard, Søren. *The Book on Adler*. Translated and edited by Howard V. Hong and Edna H. Hong. Princeton NJ: Princeton University Press, 1998.

———. *The Concept of Anxiety: A Simple Psychologically Orienting Deliberation on the Dogmatic Issue of Hereditary Sin*. Edited and translated by Reidar Thomte in collaboration with Albert B. Anderson. Princeton NJ: Princeton University Press, 1980.

———. *The Concept of Irony, with Continual Reference to Socrates*. Edited and translated by Howard V. Hong and Edna H. Hong. Princeton NJ: Princeton University Press, 1989.

———. *Concluding Unscientific Postscript to* Philosophical Fragments. Edited and translated by Howard V. Hong and Edna H. Hong. 2 volumes. Princeton NJ: Princeton University Press, 1992.

———. *Early Polemical Writings*. Edited and translated by Julia Watkin. Princeton NJ: Princeton University Press, 1990.

———. *Eighteen Upbuilding Discourses*. Edited and translated by Howard V. Hong and Edna H. Hong. Princeton NJ: Princeton University Press, 1993.

———. *Either/Or*. Edited and translated by Howard V. Hong and Edna H. Hong. 2 volumes. Princeton NJ: Princeton University Press, 1987.

———. *Fear and Trembling/Repetition*. Edited and translated by Howard V. Hong and Edna H. Hong. Princeton NJ: Princeton University Press, 1983.

———. *Journals and Papers*. Edited and translated by Howard V. Hong and Edna H. Hong. 6 volumes. Bloomington IN: Indiana University Press, 1967–1978.

———. *Kierkegaard: Samlede Værker*. Electronic edition by Alastair McKinnon. Charlottesville VA: InteLex Corporation, 1995.

———. *Philosophical Fragments/Johannes Climacus*. Edited and translated by Howard V. Hong and Edna H. Hong. Princeton NJ: Princeton University Press, 1985.

———. *The Point of View*. Edited and translated by Howard V. Hong and Edna H. Hong. Princeton NJ: Princeton University Press, 1998.

———. *Practice in Christianity*. Edited and translated by Howard V. Hong and Edna H. Hong. Princeton NJ: Princeton University Press, 1991.

———. *The Prayers of Kierkegaard*. Edited by Perry D. LeFevre. Chicago: University of Chicago Press, 1963.

———. *Sickness Unto Death: A Christian Psychological Exposition for Upbuilding and Awakening*. Translated and edited by Howard V. Hong and Edna H. Hong. Princeton NJ: Princeton University Press, 1983.

———. *Two Ages*. Edited and translated by Howard V. Hong and Edna H. Hong. Princeton NJ: Princeton University Press, 1978.

———. *Upbuilding Discourses in Various Spirits*. Edited and translated by Howard V. Hong and Edna H. Hong. Princeton NJ: Princeton University Press, 1993.

———. *Without Authority*. Edited and translated by Howard V. Hong and Edna H. Hong. Princeton NJ: Princeton University Press, 1997.

———. *Works of Love*. Edited and translated by Howard V. Hong and Edna H. Hong. Princeton NJ: Princeton University Press, 1995.

———. *Works of Love: Some Christian Reflections in the Form of Discourses*. Translated by Howard Hong and Edna Hong. New York: Harper & Row, 1962.

Kirmmse, Bruce. *Encounters with Kierkegaard: A Life as Seen by His Contemporaries*. Translated by Bruce H. Kirmmse and Virginia R. Laursen. Princeton NJ: Princeton University Press, 1996.

———. *Kierkegaard in Golden Age Denmark*. Bloomington IN: Indiana University Press, 1990.

Lamarque, Peter. "On Not Expecting Too Much from Narrative." *Mind and Language* 19 (2004): 393–408.

Lewis, C. S. *A Grief Observed*. London: Faber and Faber Press, 1963. Reprint, New York: Bantam, 1976.

Lippitt, Jon. "Getting the Story Straight: Kierkegaard, MacIntyre, and Some Problems with Narrative." *Inquiry: An Interdisciplinary Journal of Philosophy* 50 (2007): 34–69.

———. "Telling Tales: Johannes Climacus and 'Narrative Unity.'" In *Kierkegaard Studies Yearbook 2005*, edited by Niels Jørgen Cappelørn and

Hermann Deuser with K. Brian Soderquist, 71–89. New York: Walter de Gruyter, 2005.

MacIntyre, Alasdair. *After Virtue: A Study in Moral Theory*. 2nd edition. Notre Dame IN: University of Notre Dame Press, 1984.

Mansini, OSB, Guy. *Promising and the Good*. Naples FL: Sapientia Press, 2005.

McDowell, John. "Might There Be External Reasons?" In *Mind, Value, and Reality*. Cambridge MA: Harvard University Press, 1998.

Meilaender, Gilbert C. *Friendship: A Study in Theological Ethics*. Notre Dame IN: University of Notre Dame Press, 1981.

Mooney, Edward. "Getting the World Back: Kierkegaard on the *Book of Job*." In *Selves in Discord and Resolve: Kierkegaard's Moral-Religious Psychology from* Either/Or *to* Sickness Unto Death, 95–111. New York/London: Routledge, 1996.

———. "*Repetition*: Getting the World Back." In *The Cambridge Companion to Kierkegaard*, edited by Alastair Hannay and Gordon D. Marino, 282–307. Cambridge: Cambridge University Press, 1997.

Ong, SJ Walter J. "The Writer's Audience Is Always a Fiction." In *An Ong Reader: Challenges for Further Inquiry*, edited by Thomas J. Farrell and Paul A. Soukup, 405–27. Cresskill NJ: Hampton Press, Inc., 2002.

Pattison, George. "'Who' Is the Discourse? A Study in Kierkegaard's Religious Literature." *Kierkegaardiana* 16 (1993): 28–45.

Phelan, James. "Who's Here? Thoughts on Narrative Identity and Narrative Imperialism." *Narrative* 13 (2005): 205–209.

Quinn, Philip L. "Unity and Disunity, Harmony and Discord: A Response to Lillegard and Davenport." In *Kierkegaard After MacIntyre: Essays on Freedom, Narrative, and Virtue*, edited by John J. Davenport and Anthony Rudd, 327–37. Chicago IL: Open Court Publishing, 2001.

Rae, Murray. *Kierkegaard and Theology*. New York: T&T Clark, 2010.

Rawls, John. *A Theory of Justice*. Cambridge MA: The Belknap Press Harvard University Press, 1971.

Rehg, S.J., William. *Insight and Solidarity: The Discourse Ethics of Jurgen Habermas*. Los Angeles: University of California Press, 1994.

Roberts, Robert C. "Dialectical Emotions and the Virtue of Faith." In *International Kierkegaard Commentary: Concluding Unscientific Postscript to "Philosophical Fragments,"* edited by Robert L. Perkins, 73–93. Macon GA: Mercer University Press, 1997.

———. *Emotions: An Essay in Aid of Moral Psychology*. New York: Cambridge University Press, 2003.

———. "Existence, Emotion, and Virtue." In *The Cambridge Companion to Kierkegaard*, edited by Alastair Hannay and Gordon Marino, 177–206. New York: Cambridge University Press, 1998.

———. "Narrative Ethics." In *A Companion to Philosophy of Religion*, edited by Phillip L. Quinn and Charles Taliaferro, 473–80. New York: Blackwell Publishing, Ltd., 1997.

———. "Thinking Subjectively." *International Journal for Philosophy of Religion* 11 (1980): 71–92.

Rudd, Anthony. "In Defence of Narrative." *European Journal of Philosophy* 17 (2007): 60–75.

———. "Narrative, Expression, and Mental Substance." *Inquiry* 48 (2005): 413–35.

Scholes, Robert, James Phelan, and Robert Kellogg. *The Nature of Narrative*. 40th anniversary edition, revised and expanded. New York: Oxford University Press, 2006.

Stokes, Patrick. "Locke, Kierkegaard, and the Phenomenology of Personal Identity." *International Journal of Philosophical Studies* 16 / 5 (2008): 645–72.

Strawson, Galen. "Against Narrativity." *Ratio* 17 / 4 (2004): 428–52.

Taylor, Charles. *The Ethics of Authenticity*. Cambridge MA: Harvard University Press, 1991.

———. "Responsibility for Self." In *The Identities of Persons*, edited by Amelie Oksenberg

Rorty, 281–99. Berkeley CA: University of California Press, 1976.

———. *Sources of the Self: The Making of Modern Identity*. Cambridge MA: Harvard University Press, 1989.

Walsh, Sylvia. *Living Poetically: Kierkegaard's Existential Aesthetics*. University Park PA: The Pennsylvania State University Press, 1994.

Westphal, Merold. *Becoming a Self: A Reading of Kierkegaard's* Concluding Unscientific Postscript. West Lafayette IN: Purdue University Press, 1996.

———. "Commanded Love and Moral Autonomy: The Kierkegaard-Habermas Debate." In *Kierkegaard Studies Yearbook 1998*, edited by Niels Jorgen Cappelorn and Hermann Deuser with C. Stephen Evans, Alastair Hannay, and Bruce H. Kirmmse, 1–22. New York: Walter de Gruyter, 1998.

Index